# ZE



# TO

# HERO

## DIGITAL IMAGE PROCESSING

## USING MATLAB

# ZERO TO HERO

## DIGITAL IMAGE PROCESSING USING MATLAB

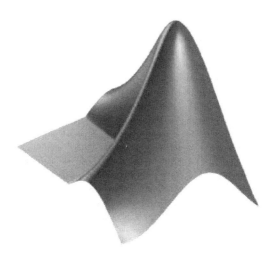

ARSATH NATHEEM S

# WHY I WROTE THIS BOOK

I wrote this book because Image processing is fresh and interesting topic for Research work. This book is all about that how to develop theory and project based notion about Image processing. This book contain plenty of programming illustration that are analyzed can also be beneficial for learners and under graduates pupils. This book starts from very basic Knowledge and gradually cover all of the improvement topics of a Image processing with MATLAB examples.

## WHY YOU SHOULD READ THIS BOOK

This book will help you learn all about digital image processing Importance, and necessity of image processing stems from application areas the first being the Improvement of data for individual interpretation and the second being that the Processing of a spectacle data for an machine perception. Digital image processing includes a assortment of applications such as remote sensing, image and information storage for transmission in acoustic imaging, medical imaging, business applications , Forensic sciences and industrial automation. Images are helpful in tracking of earth resources mapping, and forecast of urban populations, agricultural crops, climate forecasting, flooding and fire control. Space imaging applications include comprehension and analyzation of objects contained in images obtained from deep space-probe missions. There are also medical programs such as processing of X-Rays, Ultrasonic scanning, Electron micrographs, Magnetic Resonance Imaging, Nuclear Magnetic Resonance Imaging, etc.. In addition to the aforementioned applications, digital image processing is being used to solve a variety of issues. Even unrelated, these problems commonly require methods effective at improving information. The Image processing Procedures like restoration and Image enhancement are used to procedure images that were degraded or blurred. Powerful uses of image processing concepts are observed in defense astronomy, biology, medical and industrial applications. As per Medical Imaging is concerned almost all of the pictures could be utilized in the discovery of tumors or for viewing the patients. The current key field of use of digital image processing (DIP) methods is in solving the issue of machine vision so as to attain superior results

# TABLE OF CONTENTS


| CHAPTER NO | TITLE | PAGE NO |
|---|---|---|
| | Introduction | 7 |
| 1 | Basic Morphological Operation | 18 |
| | MATLAB program for dilation, erosion, opening, closing and their properties step by step explanation | 23 |
| 2 | Image Segmentation | 36 |
| | Thresholding | 37 |
| | Region, Edge based segmentation | 41 |
| | MATLAB Source Code for Image Segmentation | 55 |
| | Output for Image Segmentation | 60 |
| | Application, Conclusion | 65 |
| 3 | Intensity Transformation | 67 |
| | Theoretical Concepts: Introduction | 67 |
| | MATLAB program for Image Intensity Transformation | 74 |
| 4 | Histogram Equalization | 84 |
| | Introduction:Practical approach | 84 |
| | MATLAB Source Code for Histogram Equalization | 93 |
| | Conclusion | 104 |
| 5 | Spatial Intensity Resolution | 105 |

| | | |
|---|---|---|
| | MATLAB Source Code For Spatial Intensity Resolution | **111** |
| **6** | Enhancement in Spatial Filter | **119** |
| | MATLAB Source Code For Image Enhancement in Spatial Filtering | **127** |
| **7** | Enhancement in Frequency Filter | **134** |
| | MATLAB Source Code For Image Enhancement in Frequency Filtering | **142** |
| **8** | Color Image Processing | **149** |
| | MATLAB Source Code For Color Image Processing | **164** |
| **9** | DFT (Discrete Fourier Transform) Analysis | **180** |
| | MATLAB Source Code For DFT Analysis | **190** |
| **10** | Basic Thresholding Function | **192** |
| | MATLAB Source Code For Basic Thresholding Function | **198** |
| **11** | Sampling and Quantization | **203** |
| | MATLAB Source Code For Sampling and Quantization | **206** |
| **12** | Image Transformation | **211** |
| | MATLAB Source Code For Image Transformation | **216** |

# INTRODUCTION

## What is MATLAB?

- MATLAB = Matrix Laboratory
- "MATLAB is a high-level language and interactive environment that allows you to achieve computationally intensive tasks faster than with old-style programming languages like C, C++ and Fortran." (www.mathworks.com)
- MATLAB is an interactive, understood language that is designed for fast numerical matrix calculations

## MATLAB window components:

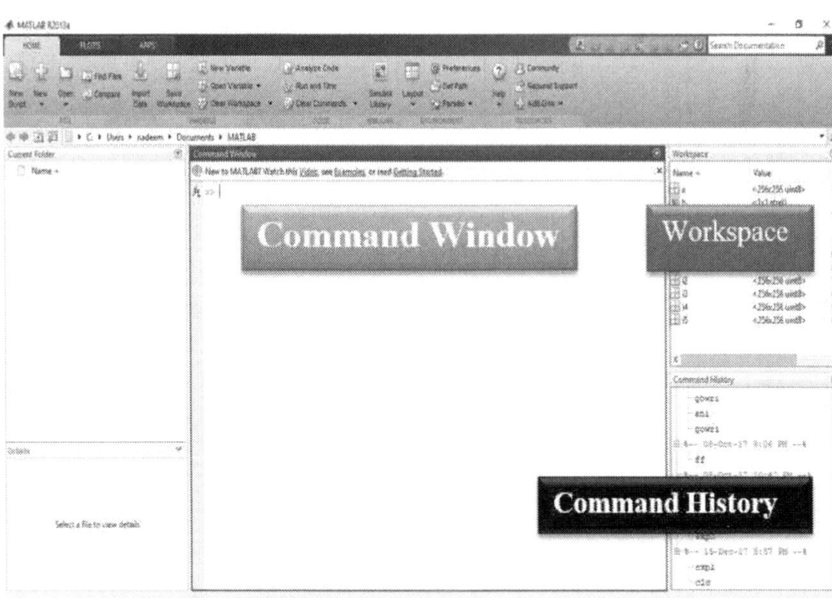

**Workspace**

Displays all the defined variables

**Command Window**

To perform commands in the MATLAB environment

**Command History**

Displays record of the commands used

**File Editor Window**

Define your functions

**MATLAB Help**

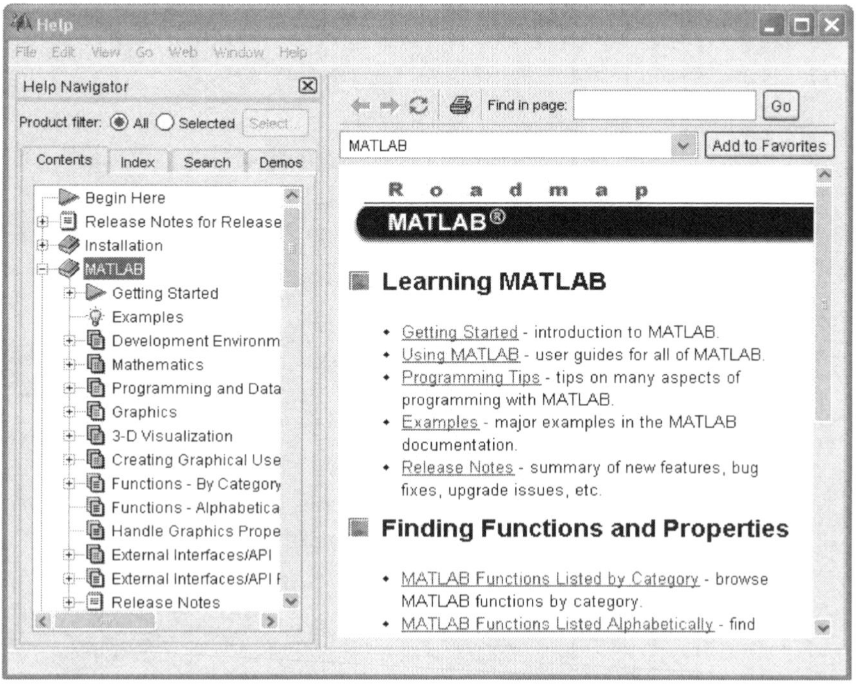

- MATLAB Help is an very powerful assistance to learning MATLAB
- Help not only contains the theoretic background, but also shows demos for implementation
- MATLAB Help can be unlocked by using the HELP pull-down menu

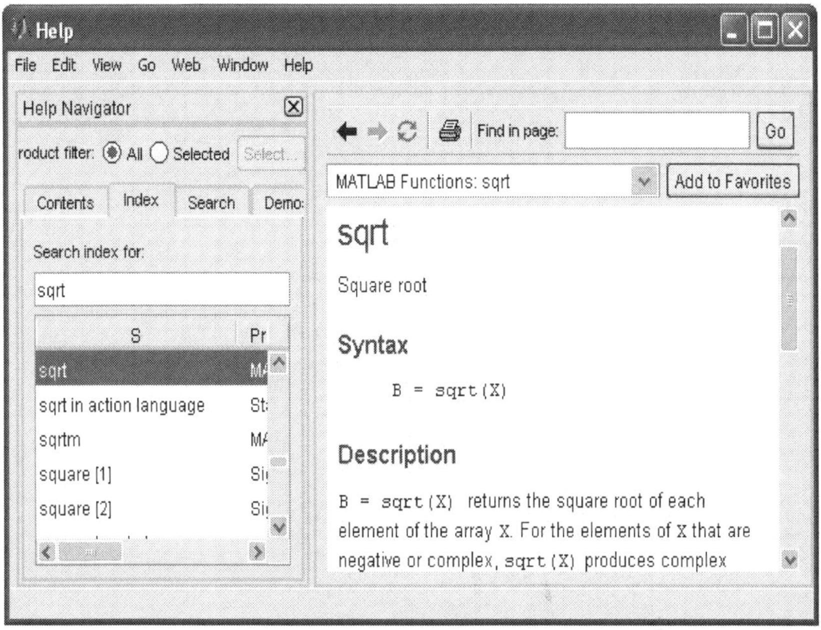


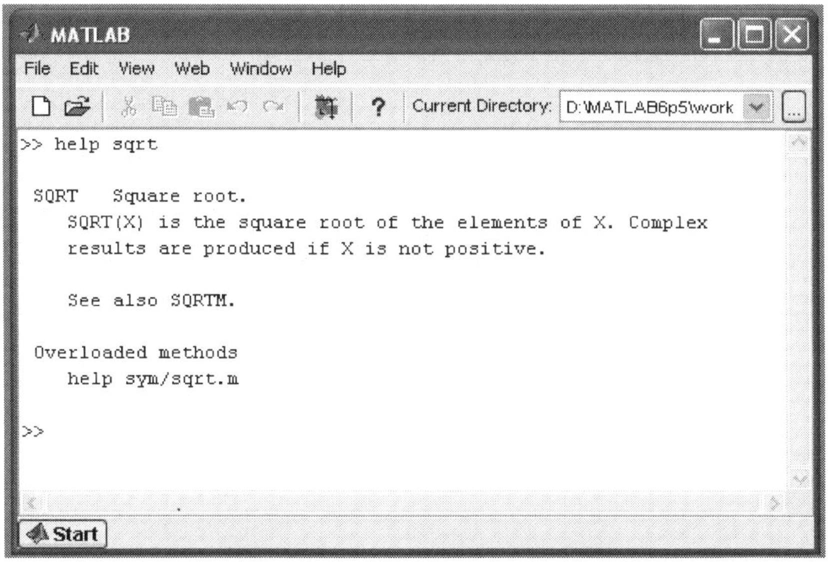

- Some command description can be found by typing the command in the search field
- As shown above, the command to take square root (SQRT) is examined
- We can also use MATLAB Help from the command window as shown

## More about the Workspace

- who, whos – present variables in the workspace
- save – save workspace variables to *.mat file
- load – load variables from *.mat file
- clear – clear workspace variables

## Matrices in MATLAB

Matrix is the main MATLAB data type

### How to build a matrix?

- A=[1 2 3; 4 5 6; 7 8 9];
- Creates matrix A of size 3 x 3

### Special matrices:

- zeros(n,m), ones(n,m), eye(n,m), rand(), randn()
- Numbers are always double (64 bits) unless you specify a dissimilar data type

**Basic Operations on Matrices**

- All operators in MATLAB are defined on matrices: +, -, *, /, ^, sqrt, sin, cos, etc.
- Element-wise operators defined by a previous dot: .*, ./, .^
- sum(A) – columns sums vector
- size(A) – size vector
- sum(sum(A)) – sum of all the elements

**Variable Name in Matlab**

✓ **Variable naming rules**

- must be **unique** in the first 63 characters

- Necessity begin with a letter

- may not contain blank spaces or additional types of punctuation

- may contain any grouping of letters, digits, and underscores

- are case-sensitive

- should not use Matlab keyword

✓ **Pre-defined variable names**

pi

**Logical Operators**

- ==, <, >, (not equal) ~=, (not) ~
- find('condition') – Returns directories of A's elements that satisfy the condition

- Example:

```
>>A=[7 3 5; 6 2 1], Idx=find(A<4)

A=

    7 3 5

    6 2 1

Idx=

    3

    4

    6
```

**Flow Control**

MATLAB has five flow control concepts:

1. if statement
2. for loop
3. while loop
4. switch statement
5. break statement

## Scripts and Functions

There are two kinds of M-files:

1. Scripts, which don't accept input opinions or return production arguments. They operate on data in the workspace
2. Functions, which can accept input opinions and return production arguments. Interior variables are local to the function

- **Example:**

A file called STAT.M:

```
function [mean, stdev]=stat(x)

%STAT Interesting statistics.

n=length(x);

mean=sum(x)/n;

stdev=sqrt(sum((x-mean).^2)/n);
```

Defines a novel function called STAT that computes the mean and standard deviation of a vector. Function name and file name should be the SAME!

## Visualization and Graphics

- plot(x,y),plot(x,sin(x)) – plot 1D function
- figure, figure(k) – open a fresh figure
- hold on, hold off – refreshing
- axis([xmin xmax ymin ymax]) – change axes
- title('figure titile') – add title to figure

- mesh(x_ax,y_ax,z_mat) – view surface
- contour(z_mat) – view z as topo map
- subplot(3,1,2) – find several plots in figure

**Saving your Effort**

```
Save mysession
```

**% creates mysession.mat with all variables**

```
Save mysession a b
```

**% save only variables a and b**

```
Clear all
```

**% clear all variables**

```
Clear a b
```

**% clear variables a and b**

```
Load my session
```

**% load session**

**What is the Image Processing Toolbox?**

- The Image Processing Toolbox is a group of functions that extend the abilities of the MATLAB's numeric scheming environment. The toolbox supports a wide range of image processing operations, together with:
    - Image analysis and enhancement
    - Geometric operations
    - Linear filtering and filter design
    - Neighborhood and block operations
    - Transforms
    - Region of interest operations
    - Binary image operations

YOU CANNOT USE THE IMAGE PROCESSING TOOLBOX FOR HOMEWORK OR FINAL PROJECT

**Images in MATLAB**

MATLAB can import/export some image formats:

- JPEG (Joint Photographic Experts Group)
- GIF (Graphics Interchange Files)
- PNG (Portable Network Graphics)
- TIFF (Tagged Image File Format)
- BMP (Microsoft Windows Bitmap)
- HDF (Hierarchical Data Format)
- PCX (Paintbrush)
- XWD (X Window Dump)

- raw-data and other types of image data
- Naturally switch images to double to achieve any processing and convert back to unsigned integer

## Data types in MATLAB

- Single (32-bit single-precision floating point)
- Double (64-bit double-precision floating point)
- Int16 (16-bit signed integer)
- Int32 (32-bit signed integer)
- Int8 (8-bit signed integer)
- Uint8 (8-bit unsigned integer)
- Uint16 (16-bit unsigned integer)
- Uint32 (32-bit unsigned integer)

## Images in MATLAB

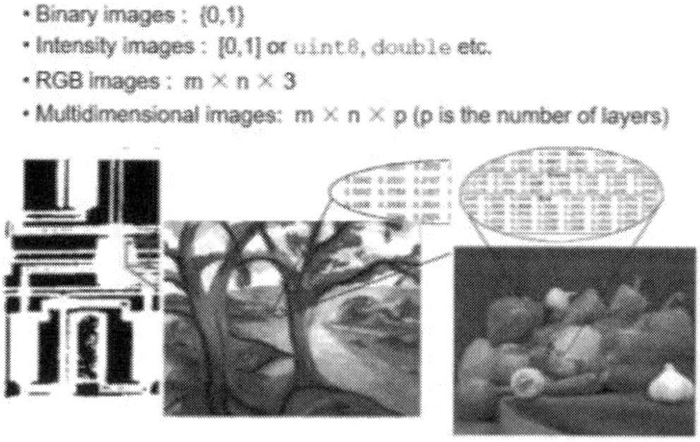

• Binary images : {0,1}
• Intensity images : [0,1] or uint8, double etc.
• RGB images : m × n × 3
• Multidimensional images: m × n × p (p is the number of layers)

## Image Import and Export

### Read and write images in Matlab

```
img = imread('apple.jpg');

dim = size(img);

figure;

imshow(img);

imwrite(img, 'output.bmp', 'bmp');
```

### Alternatives to imshow

```
imagesc(I)

imtool(I)

image(I)
```

### Image Display

- imshow - display image
- image - create and display image object
- imagesc - scale and display as image

# CHAPTER 1.

## BASIC MORPHOLOGICAL OPERATION

### Introduction

Image Processing is a technique to perform some functions on an image, in order to have an improved image or to extract various interesting facts from it. Image Morphology is an essential tool in image processing. It is actually the learn shapes of object present in the image and extraction of image features. Image features are essential for object recognition. The basic morphological operations include Erosion and Dilation, Opening and Closing are also morphological operators. These operators are deciding on as basic operations in image processing algorithms.

### DILATION

Dilation operator can be used to binary and grey scale images. The purpose of this operator is to expand the window and shrinks background. It slowly increases the boundaries of the region, while the small holes existing in the image become smaller. It increases the illumination of the object.

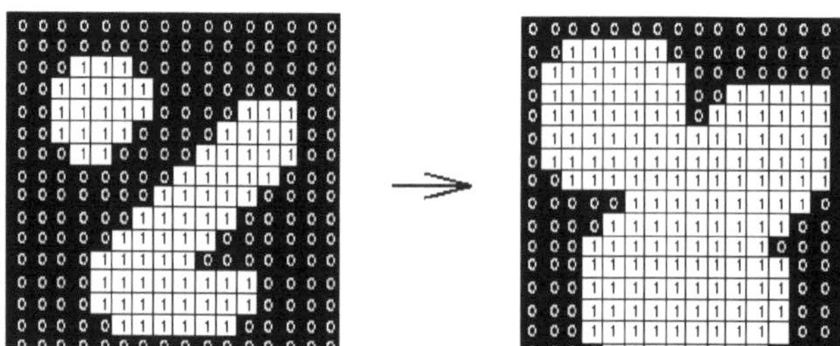

Fig.1.Example: Dilation

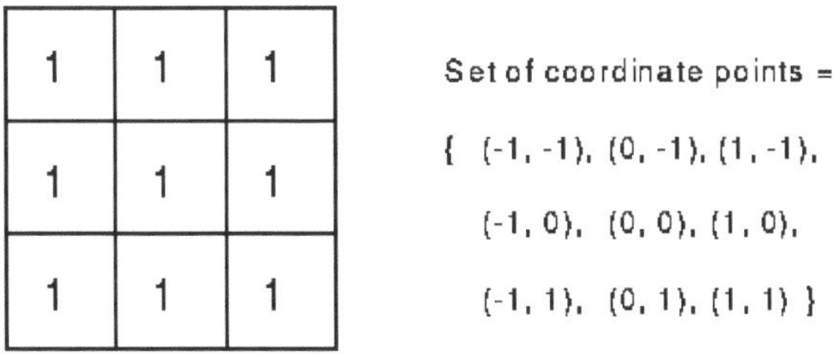


Fig.1.1. Applied Structuring Element

## EROSION

Erosion is significant operation. The purpose of erosion operators is to shrinks the window and grows background. Erosion is used to make an object shorter by eliminating is outside region of pixels. After implementing the erosion operator on the image, the image gets darker. This particular operator will take the image and structuring element as inputs and thins the subject.

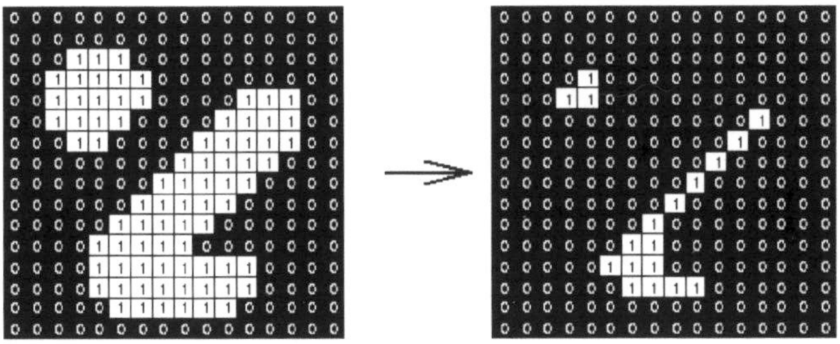

Fig.1.2.Example: Erosion

| | | |
|---|---|---|
| 1 | 1 | 1 |
| 1 | 1 | 1 |
| 1 | 1 | 1 |

Set of coordinate points =

{ (-1, -1), (0, -1), (1, -1),

(-1, 0), (0, 0), (1, 0),

(-1, 1), (0, 1), (1, 1) }

Fig.1.3. Applied Structuring Element

**OPENING**

Opening operation is mixed of dilation and erosion operations. If A and are two sets of pixels, then in the opening, 1st erode A by B then dilate the result by B. Opening is the union of all B objects

Totally contained in A.

- Similar to Erosion
- Spot and noise removal
- Less destructive
- Erosion next dilation
- The similar structuring element for both operations.

**Input:**

- Binary Image
- Structuring Element.

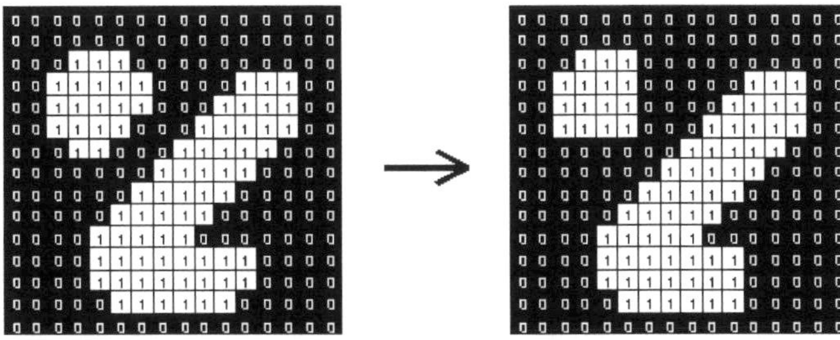

Fig.1.4.Example: Opening

- Choose the structuring element (SE) and move it around inside each highlight area.
- All highlight pixels which cannot be accessed by the structuring element without lapping over the edge of the feature object will be eroded away
- All pixels which can be protected by the SE with the SE being completely within the highlight region will be preserved.
- Opening is idempotent, repeating application has no further impact

## CLOSING

Closing operation is a dilation operation adopted by an erosion operation. Closing is actually the group of points, which the intersection of object B about them with object A is not vacant.

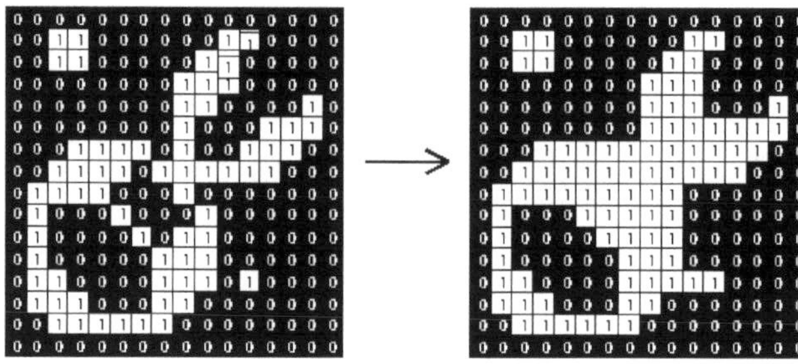

Fig.1.5. Example: Closing

- Choose the structuring element (SE) and move it around outside each highlight area.
- All background pixels which can be protected by the SE with the structuring element to be entirely within the background area will be preserved.
- All background pixels which can't be achieved by the structuring element without lapping over the edge of the window object will be turned into a foreground.
- Opening is idempotent: repeating application has no additional effects

# MATLAB PROGRAM FOR DILATION, EROSION, OPENING, CLOSING AND THEIR PROPERTIES

**SOURCE** CODE:

```
clc;

clear all;

close all;

a=imread('C:\Users\natheem\Desktop\images\India_satellite.png');

% Read an input image


b=strel('line',11,90);

% strel represents morphological structuring element


figure(1);

imshow(a);

title('Original image');


c=imdilate(a,b);

figure(2);

imshow(c);

title('Dilate image');
```

```
d=strel('disk',11);
e=imerode(a,d);
figure(3);
imshow(e);
title('Erode image')

c=imopen(a,b);
figure(4);
imshow(c);
title('Open image');

d=strel('disk',11);
e=imclose(a,d);
figure(5);
imshow(e);
title('Close image')

%Properties
h=[0 1 0;1 1 1;0 1 0];
```

```
i1=imdilate(a,h);

figure(6);

imshow(i1);

title('Dilate image pro1'); % pro=properties


i2=imerode(a,h);

figure(7);

imshow(i2);

title('Erode image ');


i3=a-i2;

figure(8);

imshow(i3);

title('pro3');


i4=i1-a;

figure(9);

imshow(i4);

title('pro4');
```

```
i5=i1-i2;

figure(10);

imshow(i5);

title('pro5');
```

STEP BY STEP EXPLANATION

**STEP 1:** Type Program on MATLAB comment window

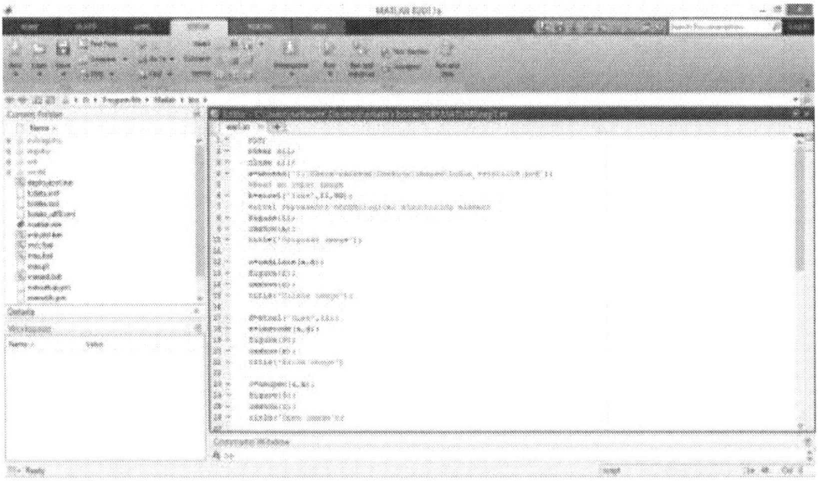

**STEP 2:** Save program & Run Program Click 'Add to path'

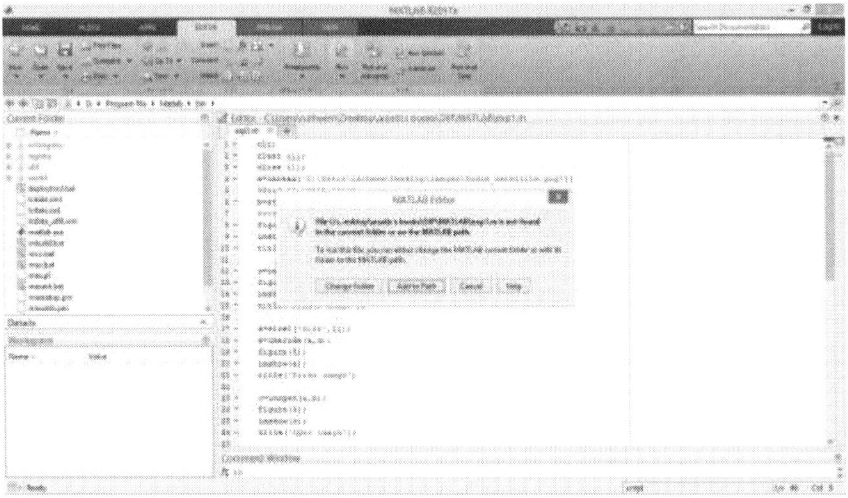

**STEP 3:** You will get Corresponding Output for Morphological Operation

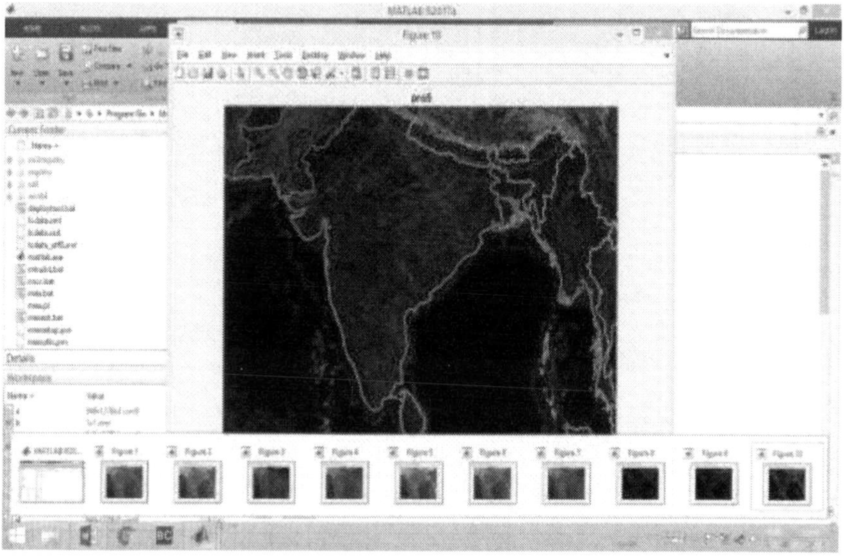

## RESULT:

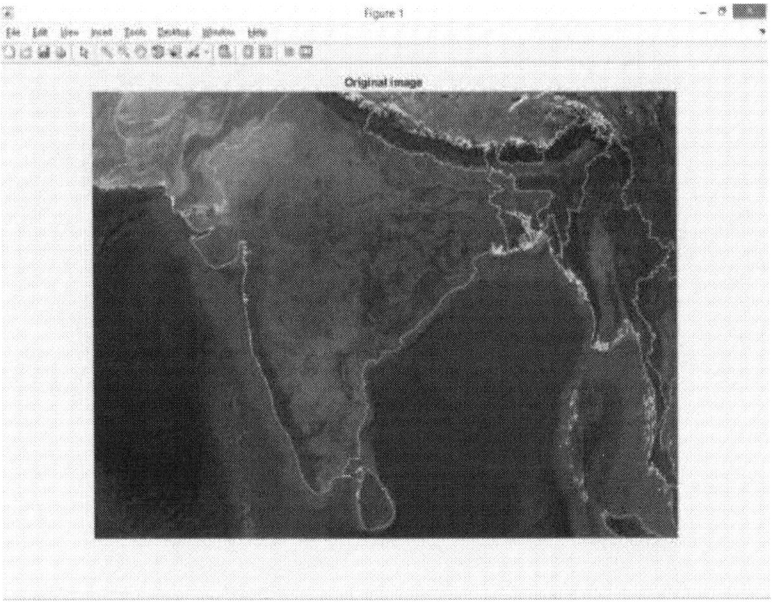


Fig.1.Orignal Image

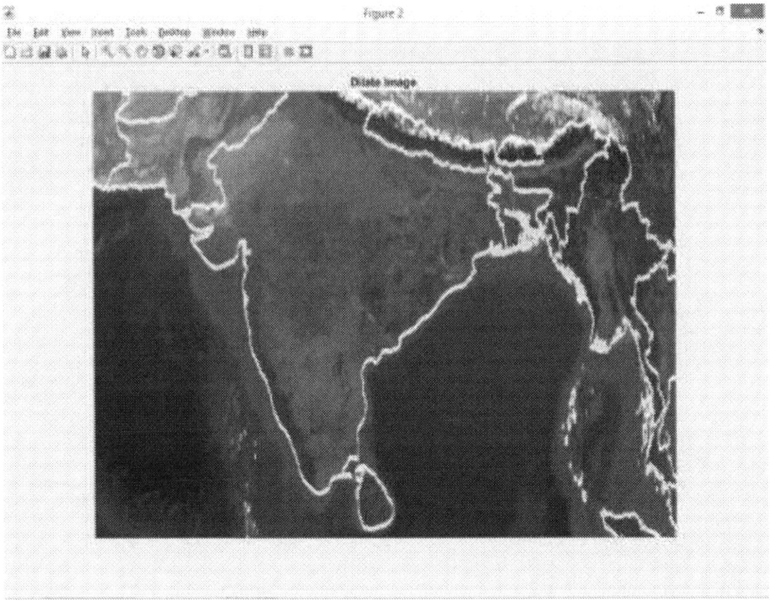


Fig.2.Dialating Image

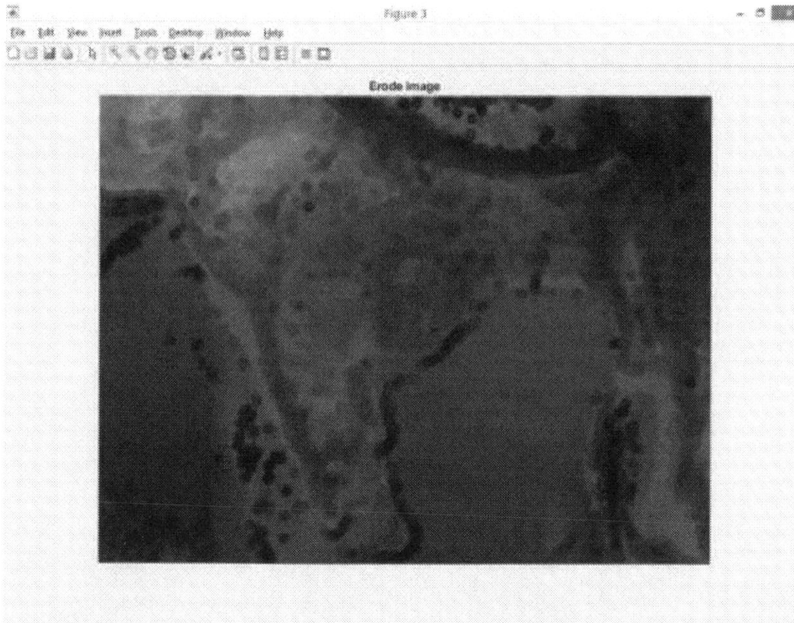


Fig.3.Eroded Image

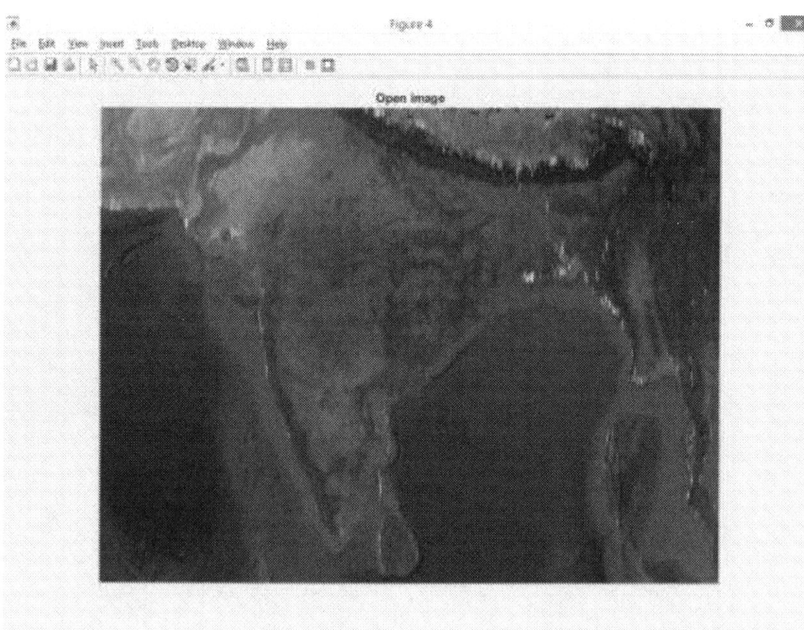


Fig.4.Opening Image

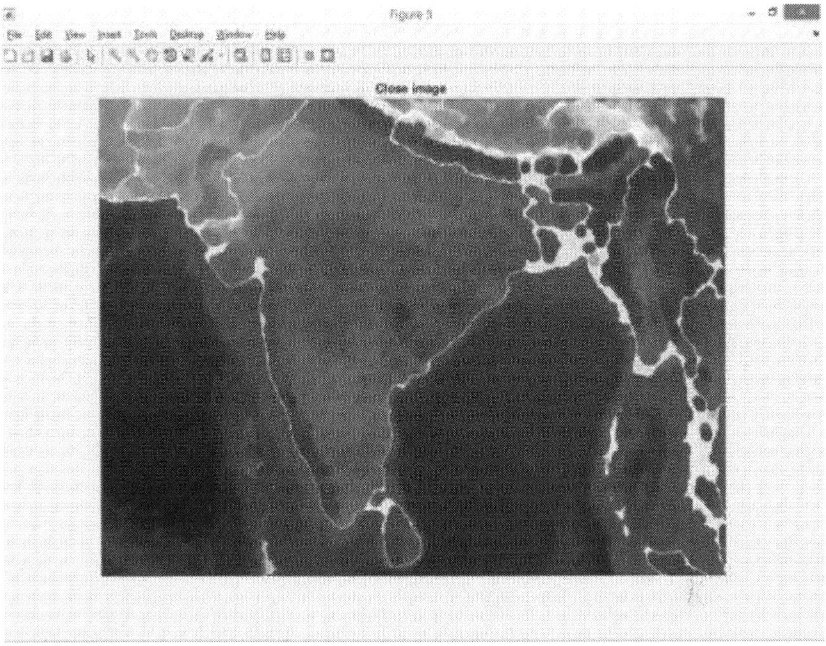


Fig.5.Closing Image

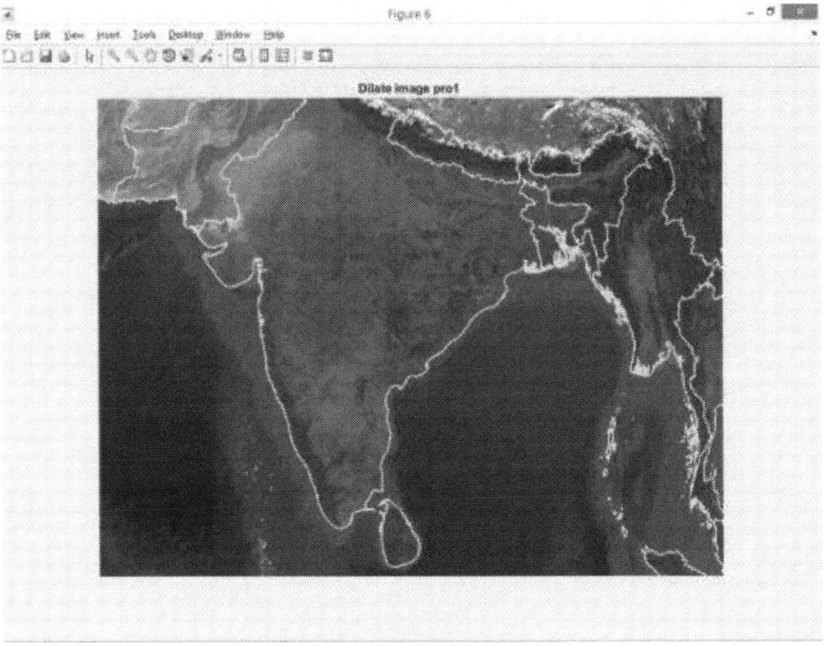


Fig.6.Dialate Image property 1

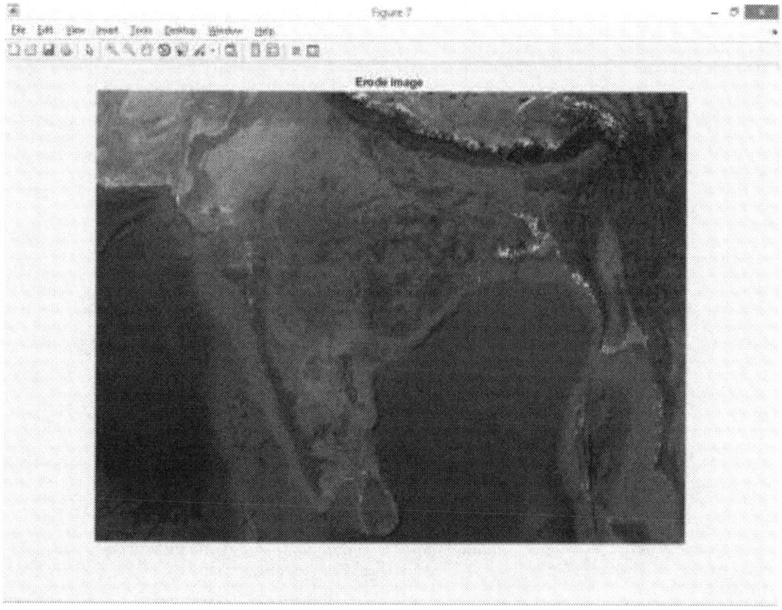


Fig.7.Erode Image property 2

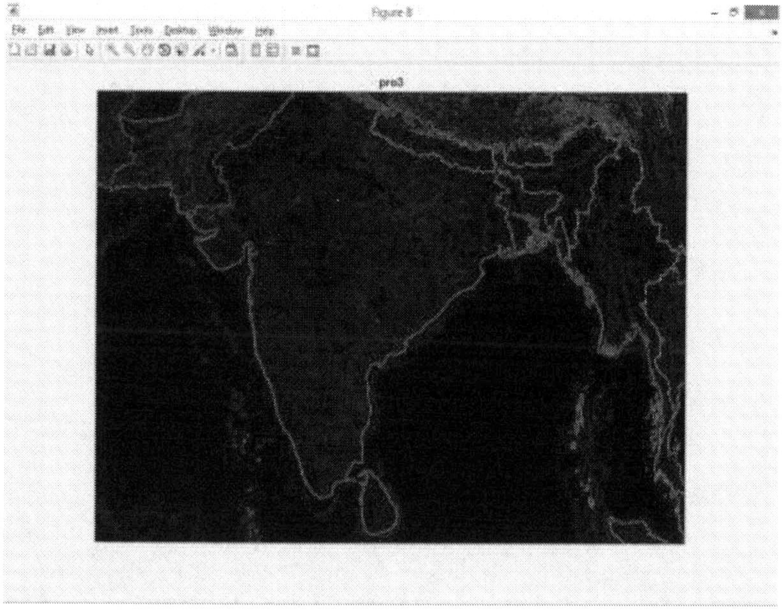


Fig.8. property 3

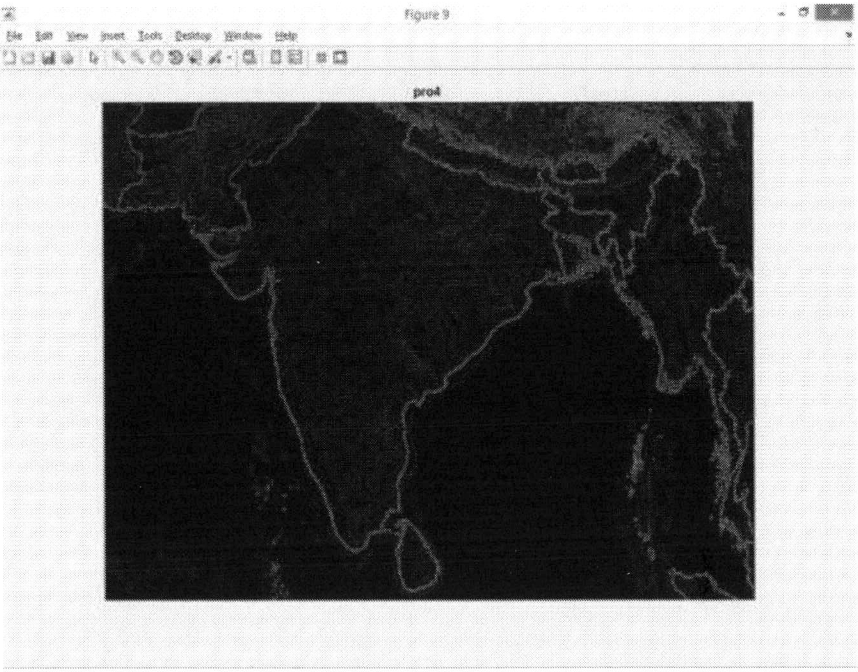


Fig.9. property 1

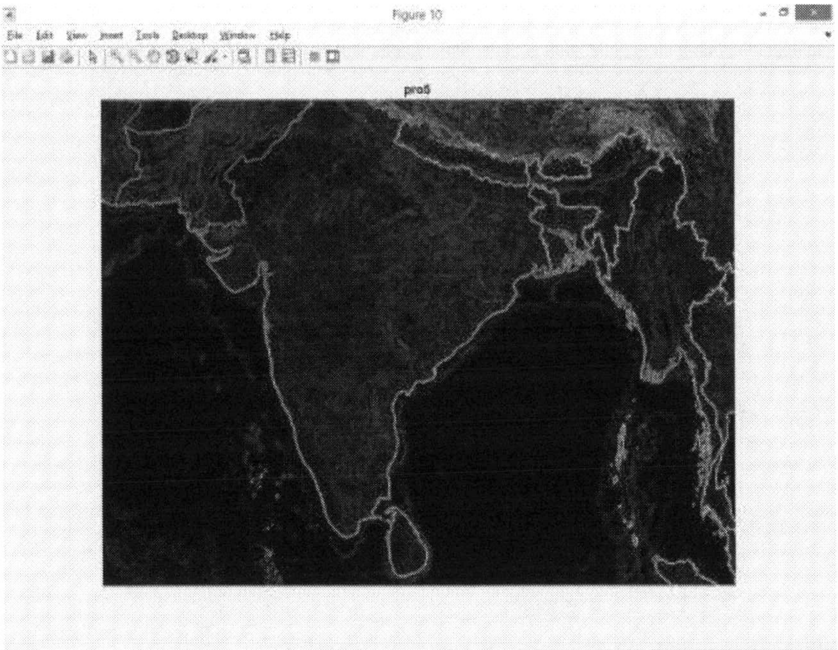


Fig.5.Dialate Image property 1

## FUTURE SCOPE

The Morphological Image Processing can be further applied to a wide range of problems including

- **Medical image analysis:**
    - Tumour detection,
    - Regurgitation,
    - Measurement of size and shape of interior organs.

- **Robotics:**

    Recognition and understanding of objects in a scene, motion control and implementation through visual feedback

- **Radar imaging:**
    - Target detection and identification.
    - Selection of Structuring element for object classification over morphology is still interesting to this technique and has been chosen to be the main direction of the future work.

## APPLICATIONS

Morphology is applied as a technique for image transformation. It has been utilized for extraction of edges and detection of the attribute objects in mobile photogrammetric techniques to making maps from images taken from a car, named mobile mapping systems Morphology is used primarily for decrease an region of interest and extracting particular objects like street signals. Features of morphology are also used in discovering sewer pipelines problems. Architectural commemorations as well as industrial things have edges and areas which can be probably detected by use of mathematical morphology functions.

## CONCLUSION

The handling of image is faster as well as more cost effective. Morphological image processing characterized an image processing technique which compact with the form of features in an image. in this chapter use of morphological operators are described with morphological algorithms. This section highlighted the Morphological operations like as Dilation, Erosion, and Opening, Closing and morphological processes like Boundary Extraction,

Thickening, thinning, Noise elimination and pruning which are really helpful process or implement any image. Most Application areas of image processing tend to be Medical imaging, Industrial automated, Biometrics, Cinematography, Armed Application. Image Processing applications are existing in all area.

# CHAPTER 2.

## IMAGE SEGMENTATION

**What is segmentation?**

Image segmentation is the process of partitioning an image into a collection of connected sets of pixels. The goal of segmentation is to simplify change the representation of an image into something that is more meaningful and easier to analyses. Image segmentation is typically used to locate objects and boundaries like lines, curves in images. It is the process of assigning a label to every pixel in an image.

**Three main techniques to do.**

1. Thresholding
2. Region based segmentation
3. Edge based segmentation

# THRESHOLDING

Thresholding is finding histogram of gray level intensity.

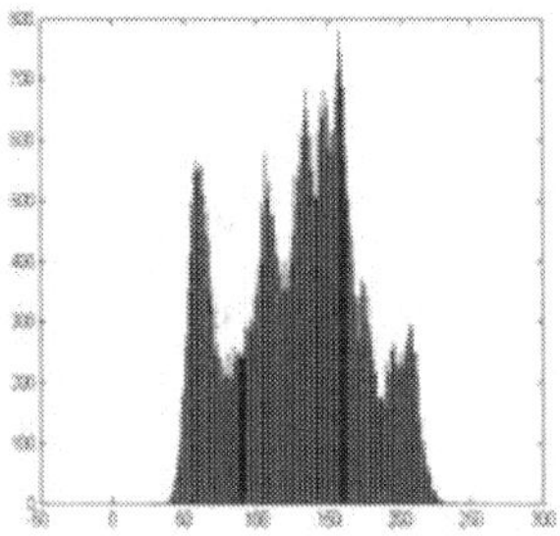

**Types**

1. Basic Global Thresholding
2. Multiple Threshold
3. Variable Thresholding
4. Otsu's Technique

**Basic Global Thresholding**

- Primarily Segment image use:

$$g(x,y) = \begin{cases} 1 & \text{if } f(x,y) \geq T \\ 0 & \text{if } f(x,y) \leq T \end{cases}$$

- Calculate the average intensity **m1** and **m2** for the pixels

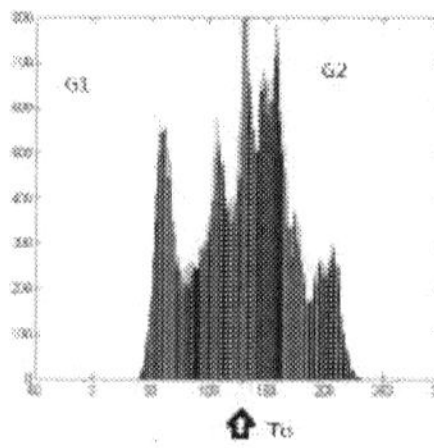


- Calculate a fresh threshold:

$$T = \frac{1}{2}(m_1 + m_2)$$

- Until the variance between values of T is minor than a predefined parameter.

**Otsu's Technique**

- Based on a very simple idea: Find the threshold that minimizes the weighted within-class variance.
- This turns out to be the same as maximizing the between-class variance.
- Operates directly on the gray level histogram.

**Multiple Threshold**

As Otsu's technique, it takes extra area and k*

$$\sigma_B^2 = P_1(m_1 - m_G)^2 + P_2(m_2 - m_G)^2 + P_3(m_3 - m_G)^2$$

$$P_1 m_1 + P_2 m_2 + P_3 m_3 = m_G$$

$$P_1 + P_2 + P_3 = 1$$

$$\sigma_B^2(k_1^*, k_2^*) = \max_{0<k_1<k_2<L-1} \sigma_B^2(k_1, k_2)$$

$$\eta(k_1^*, k_2^*) = \frac{\sigma_B^2(k_1^*, k_2^*)}{\sigma_G^2}$$

**Disadvantage:**

It becomes too complex when amount of region more than two or three.

**Variable Thresholding**

1) Image partitioning

It is work once the objects of interest and the background inhabit areas of sensibly similar size. If not, it will fail.

2) Variable thresholding based on local image properties

3) By moving average

It debated is based on computing a moving average along scan appearances of an image.

$$m(k+1) = \frac{1}{n} \sum_{i=k+2-n}^{k+1} z_i = m(k) + \frac{1}{n}(z_{k+1} - z_{k-n})$$

$$g(x,y) = \begin{cases} 1 & \text{if } Q(\text{local parameters}) \text{ is true} \\ 0 & \text{if } Q(\text{local parameters}) \text{ is true} \end{cases}$$

$$Q(\sigma_{xy}, m_{xy}) = \begin{cases} \mathit{true} & \text{if } f(x,y) > a\sigma_{xy} \text{ AND } f(x,y) > bm_{xy} \\ \mathit{false} & \text{otherwise} \end{cases}$$

# REGION BASED SEGMENTATION

Region Segmentation is procedure of finding region, but not finding edge

1. Region Growing
2. Cheng-Jin Kuo`s method is used
3. Data Grouping (Clustering Technique)
4. Partitional clustering

**Algorithm:**

- Select a random pixels
- Usage 8-connected and threshold to decide
- Repeat a and b until nearly points are classified.

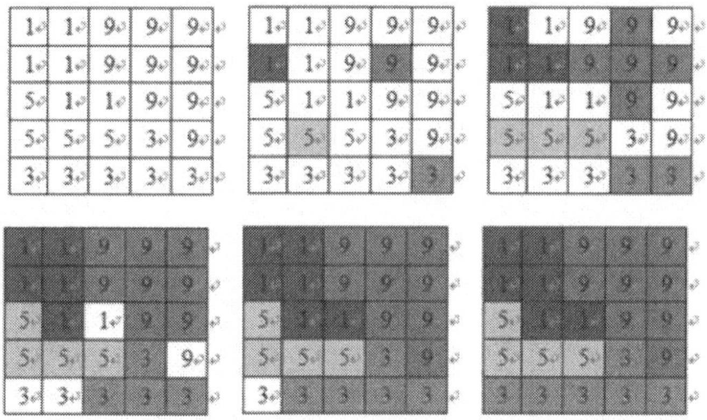

- Reproduction of region growing (90% pixels )

Threshold/second: 20/4.7 seconds.

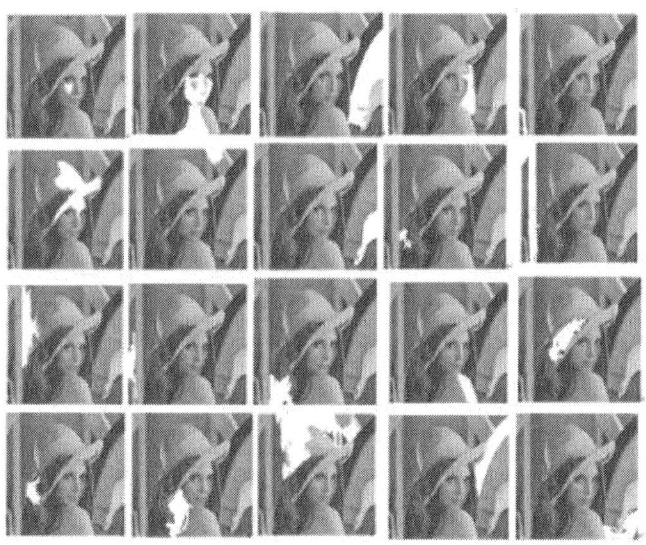

**Data Clustering**

- Using centroid to signify the huge amounts of clusters
- Partitional clustering, we have to choose the number of clustering we want first before we begin the process.
- Hierarchical clustering, we can alteration the number of cluster anytime throughout process if we need.

**Hierarchical clustering**

1) **Algorithm of hierarchical accumulation (built)**
   - Understand every solo data as a cluster **Ci**
   - Find out **Ci**, **Cj** for the distance is the shortest.
   - Repeat the steps until satisfies our request.
   - **d(a,b)** as the space between data **a** and **b**
2) **Algorithm of hierarchical division (break up )** :

Diameter of cluster

$$D(C_i) = \max(d(\text{a},\text{b}))\ , for\ \forall \text{a} \in C_i\ , \forall \text{b} \in C_i$$

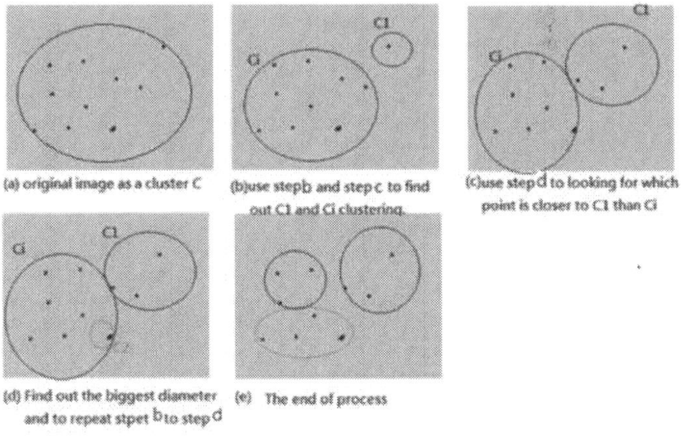


(a) original image as a cluster C (b)use step b and step c to find out C1 and Ci clustering. (c)use step d to looking for which point is closer to C1 than Ci (d) Find out the biggest diameter and to repeat stpet b to step d (e) The end of process

## Partitional clustering

Choose the numbers of the cluster (k-means)

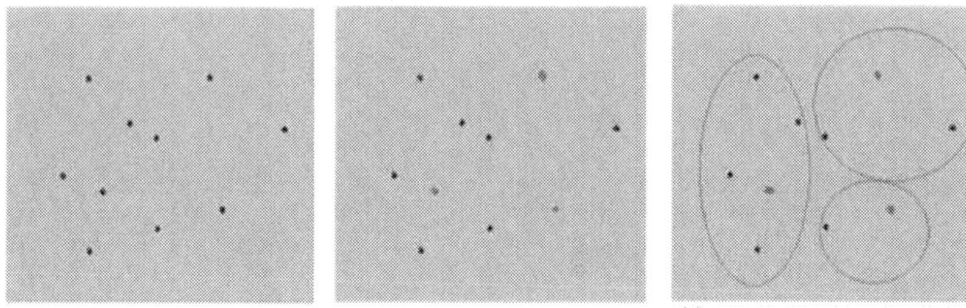

## ADVANTAGES & DISADVANTAGES

### Hierarchical algorithm

Advantages

- Result is reliable
- Idea is simple

Disadvantages

- It is consuming, so is not suitable for a big database.

### Partitional algorithms

Advantages

- Numbers of cluster is fixed, so the concept is also simple.
- Calculating speed is fast.

Disadvantages

- Determine the number of clusters.
- Initial problem

## Edge-Based Segmentation

Edge-Based Segmentation is by mask to notice edge in image by convolution.

1. Basic Edge Detection
2. SRHLT - Short response Hilbert transform
3. Watersheds
4. The Marr Hildreth edge detector (LoG)

## Basic Edge Detection

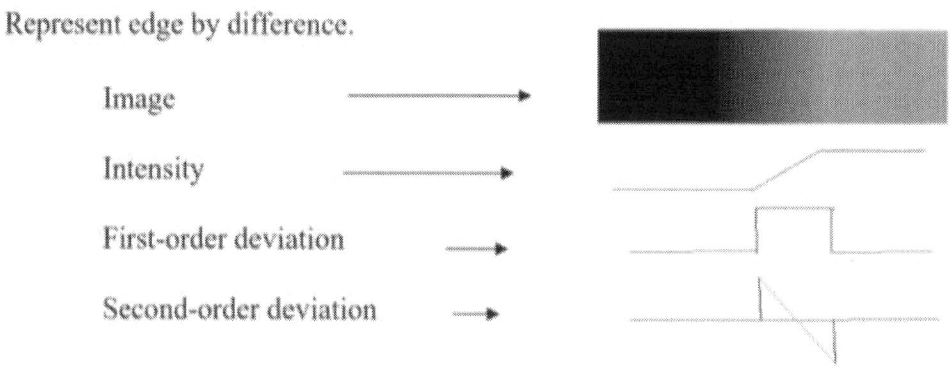

**Gradient**

- Gradient is to find edge strength and direction at site $(x,y)$ of image.

$$\nabla f \equiv \text{grad}(f) \equiv \begin{bmatrix} g_x \\ g_y \end{bmatrix} = \begin{bmatrix} \frac{\partial f}{\partial x} \\ \frac{\partial f}{\partial y} \end{bmatrix}$$

- The magnitude of vector, meant as M(x,y)

$$\text{mag}(\nabla f) = \sqrt{g_x + g_y}$$

- The direction of the gradient vector is assumed by the angle

$$\alpha(x, y) = \tan^{-1}\left[\frac{g_y}{g_x}\right]$$

**Roberts**

Robert edge detection, the perpendicular and horizontal edges carry out separately and then place together for resulting edge detection. The Roberts edge detector uses the next masks to approximate digitally the first derivatives as differences between adjacent pixels.

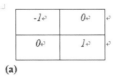

| | |
|---|---|
| -1 | 0 |
| 0 | 1 |

(a)

| | |
|---|---|
| 0 | -1 |
| 1 | 0 |

(b)

**Prewitt operator**

Prewitt operator edge detection masks are the one of the oldest and greatest understood methods of detecting edges in images The Prewitt edge detector uses the following mask to approximate digitally the first derivatives Gx and Gy.

| | | |
|---|---|---|
| -1 | -1 | -1 |
| 0 | 0 | 0 |
| 1 | 1 | 1 |

(c)

| | | |
|---|---|---|
| -1 | 0 | 1 |
| -1 | 0 | 1 |
| -1 | 0 | 1 |

(d)

| | | |
|---|---|---|
| 0 | 1 | 1 |
| -1 | 0 | 1 |
| -1 | -1 | 0 |

(e)

| | | |
|---|---|---|
| -1 | -1 | 0 |
| -1 | 0 | 1 |
| 0 | 1 | 1 |

(f)

**Sobel operator**

The sobel edge detector calculates the gradient by using the discrete differences between rows and columns of a 3X3 neighborhood. The sobel operator is based on convolving the image with a minor, divisible, and number valued filter.

$$G(x,y) = \begin{cases} 1 & \text{if } |R(x,y)| \geq T \\ 0 & \text{otherwise} \end{cases}$$

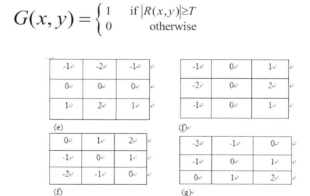

| | | |
|---|---|---|
| -1 | -2 | -1 |
| 0 | 0 | 0 |
| 1 | 2 | 1 |

(e)

| | | |
|---|---|---|
| -1 | 0 | 1 |
| -2 | 0 | 2 |
| -1 | 0 | 1 |

(f)

| | | |
|---|---|---|
| 0 | 1 | 2 |
| -1 | 0 | 1 |
| -2 | -1 | 0 |

(f)

| | | |
|---|---|---|
| -2 | -1 | 0 |
| -1 | 0 | 1 |
| 0 | 1 | 2 |

(g)

## Canny Edge Detection

Canny edge detection is a multistage algorithm to detect a extensive range of edges in images. This detector finds edges by observing for local maxima of the gradient off (x, y). The gradient is calculated using the derivative of a Gaussian filter. The technique uses two thresholds to detect strong and weak edges and includes the weak edges in the output only if they are connected to strong edges

## The Marr-Hildreth edge detector (LoG)

This is second-order deviation, known as Laplacian.

| | | | | |
|---|---|---|---|---|
| 0 | 0 | -1 | 0 | 0 |
| 0 | -1 | -2 | -1 | 0 |
| -1 | -2 | 16 | -2 | -1 |
| 0 | -1 | -2 | -1 | 0 |
| 0 | 0 | -1 | 0 | 0 |

Filter the input image with an *n*n* Gaussian low pass filter. 99.7% of the capacity under a 2-D Gaussian surface lies between around the mean.

$$g(x, y) = [\nabla^2 G(x, y)] \otimes f(x, y)$$

$$\downarrow$$

$$g(x, y) = \nabla^2 [G(x, y) \otimes f(x, y)]$$

**Short response Hilbert Transform (SRHLT)**

**1) Hilbert transform**

$$g_H(\tau) = h(x) * g(x), \quad \text{where } h(x) = \frac{1}{\pi x}$$

$$G_H(f) = H(f)G(f) \qquad H(f) = -j\,\mathrm{sgn}(f)$$

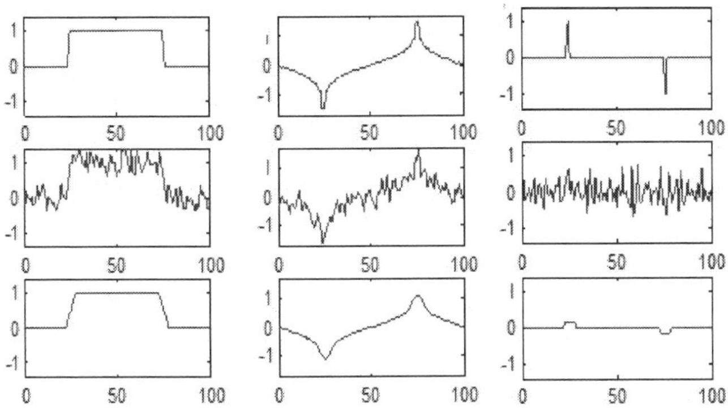


**2)** Short response Hilbert transform **(SRHLT)**

$$g_H(\tau) = h_b(x) * g(x), \quad \text{where } h_b(x) = |b|\,\mathrm{csch}(\pi b x)$$

$$G_H(f) = H_b(f)G(f) \;\text{ where } G_H(f) = FT[g_H(\tau)],$$
$$G(f) = FT[g(\tau)], \qquad H_b(f) = -j\tanh(\pi f / b).$$

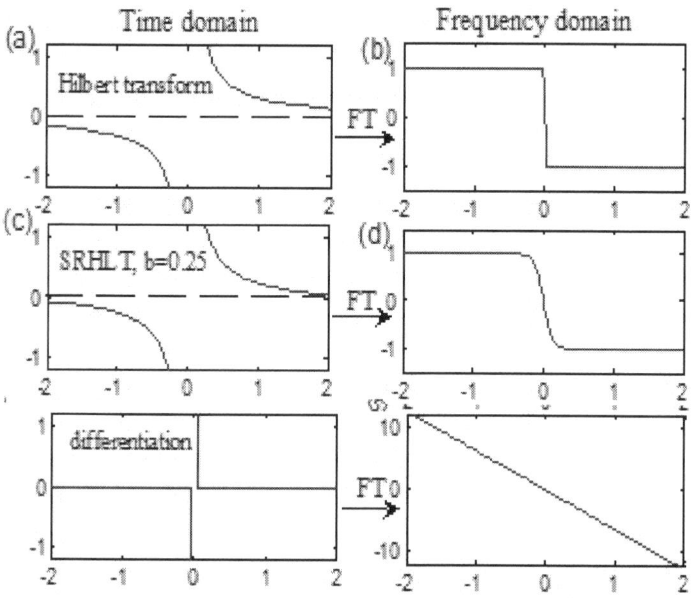
Time domain
Frequency domain
(a)
(b)
Hilbert transform
FT
(c)
(d)
SRHLT, b=0.25
FT
differentiation
FT

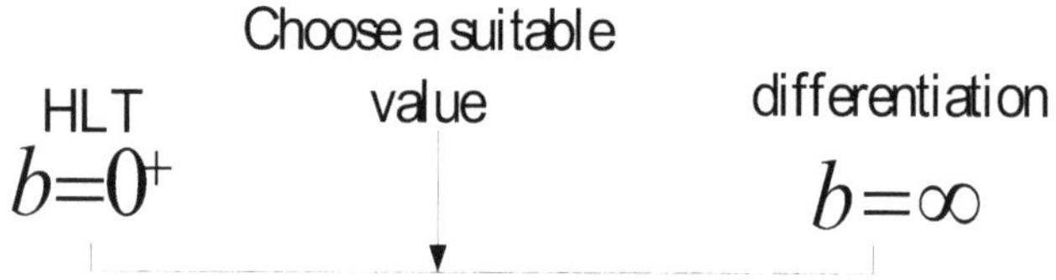
Choose a suitable value
HLT
$b=0^+$
differentiation
$b=\infty$

# Watersheds

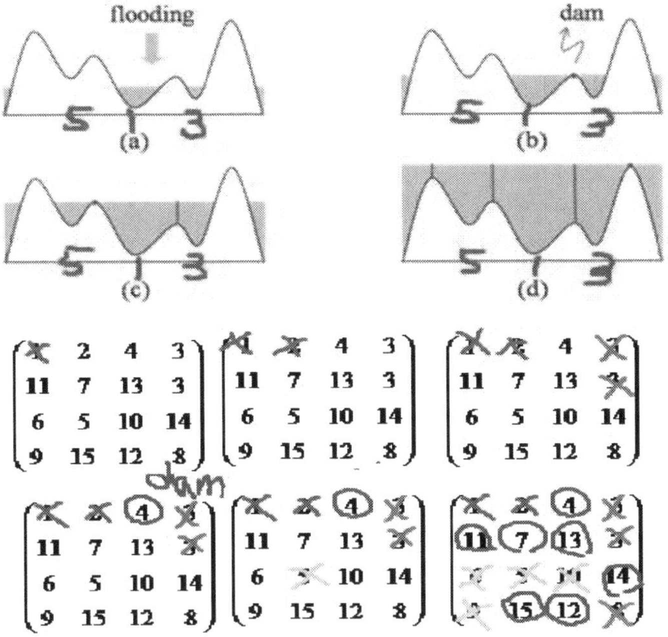


## Algorithm:

$$T[n] = \{(s,t) \mid g(s,t) < n\}$$ g(s,t) is intensity.

n= min+1 to n = max +1. And let T[n]=0, others 1.

$$C[n] = \bigcup_{i=1}^{R} C_n(M_i)$$ $C_n(M_i)$ is minimum point beneath n.

## Markers

### Outside markers:

- Points along the watershed line along maximum points.

### Interior markers:

- All points in connected component have the similar intensity.
- Points in area form a connected component
- That is surrounded higher points.

## MATLAB CODE FOR IRIS SEGMENTATION

Iris segmentation is very significant for an iris recognition system. If the iris regions were not properly segmented, there would possibly exist four kinds of noises in segmented iris areas: eyelashes, eyelids, reflections and pupil, which will outcome in poor recognition performance. This paper proposes a new noise-removing method, Founded on the fusion of edge and region data.

## THE ENTIRE PROCEDURE INCLUDES 3 STEPS:

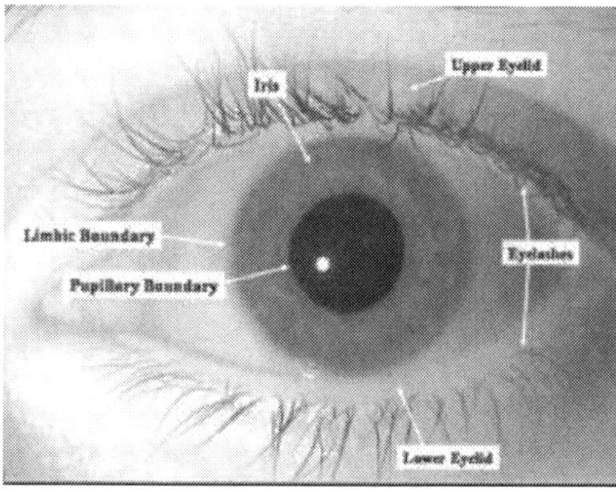


1) Irregular localization and normalization,
2) Edge data extraction based on phase congruency, and
3) The infusion of edge and region data

## MATLAB GUI for Iris Segmentation

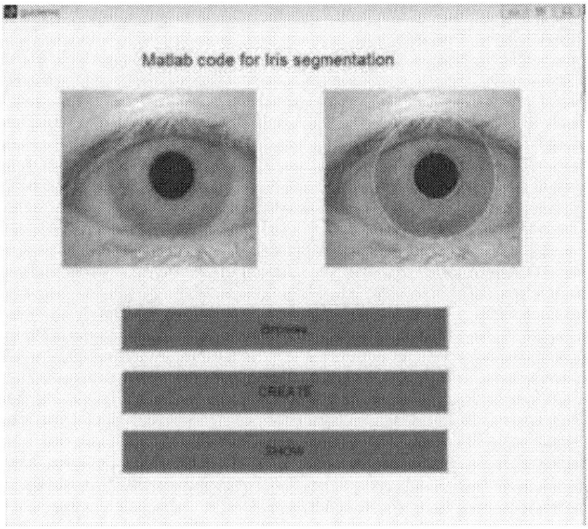


## MATLAB CODE FOR IRIS SEGMENTATION

Here you can download this code from this link

https://www.pantechsolutions.net/image-processing-projects/matlab-code-for-iris-segmentation

MATLAB code for K-means Segmentation

https://www.dropbox.com/s/um4zhhb5qhfj9kt/matlab_code_for_k_means_segmentation.rar?dl=0bb

**Flow Chart**

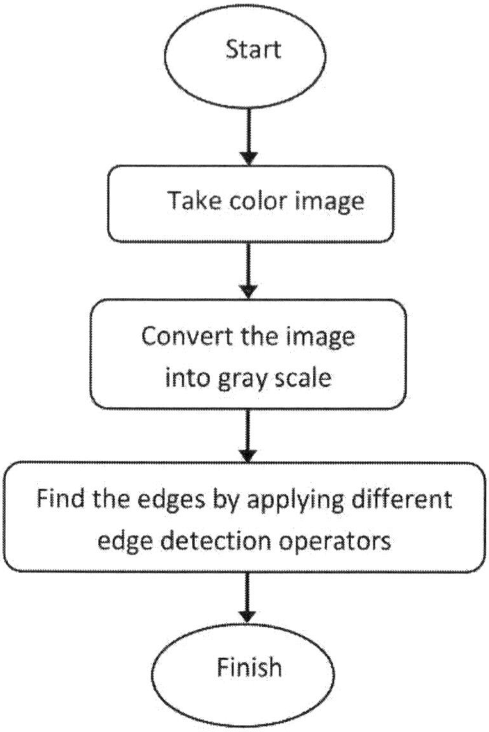


```
%IMAGE SEGMENTATION

clc;

clear all;

close all;

%edge detection

a=imread('autumn.tif');

b=rgb2gray(a);
```

```
figure(1);

imshow(b);

title('original image');


%roberts operator

c=edge(b,'roberts');

figure(2);

imshow(c);

title('roberts image');


%sobel operator

d=edge(b,'sobel');

figure(3);

imshow(d);

title('sobel image');


%prewitt operator

e=edge(b,'prewitt');

figure(4);

imshow(e);
```

```
title('prewitt image');

%log operator

f=edge(b,'log');

figure(5);

imshow(f);

title('log image');


%canny operator

g=edge(b,'canny');

figure(6);

imshow(g);

title('canny image');


%point detection

h=[0,1,0;1,-4,1;0,1,0];

i=imfilter(b,h,'symmetric','conv');

figure(7);

imshow(i);

title('laplacian point filtered image');
```

```
%line detection

j=im2bw(b);

w=(1/3)*[1,0,-1;1,0,-1;1,0,-1];

k=imfilter(double(j),w);

k(k<1)=0;

figure(8);

imshow(k);

title('line detection image');
```

# OUTPUT FOR IMAGE SEGMENTATION

**Fig.1** Original Image

**Fig.2.** Gray Scale image

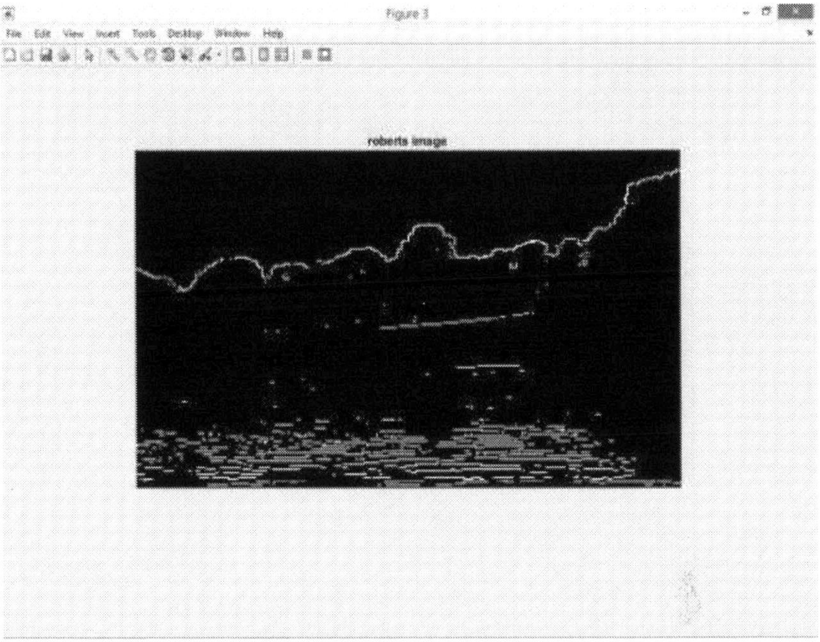


**Fig.3.** Robert image

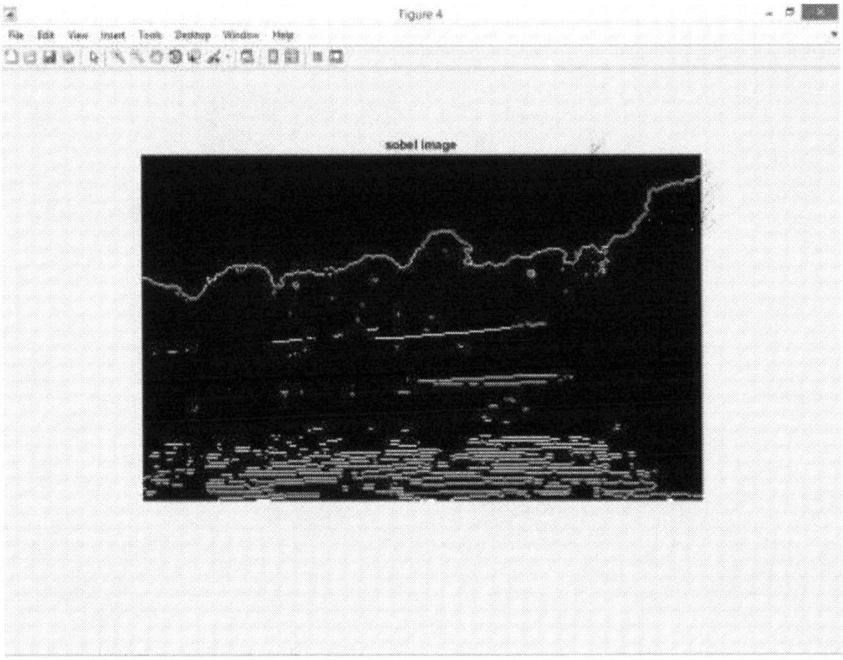


**Fig.4.** Sobel Image

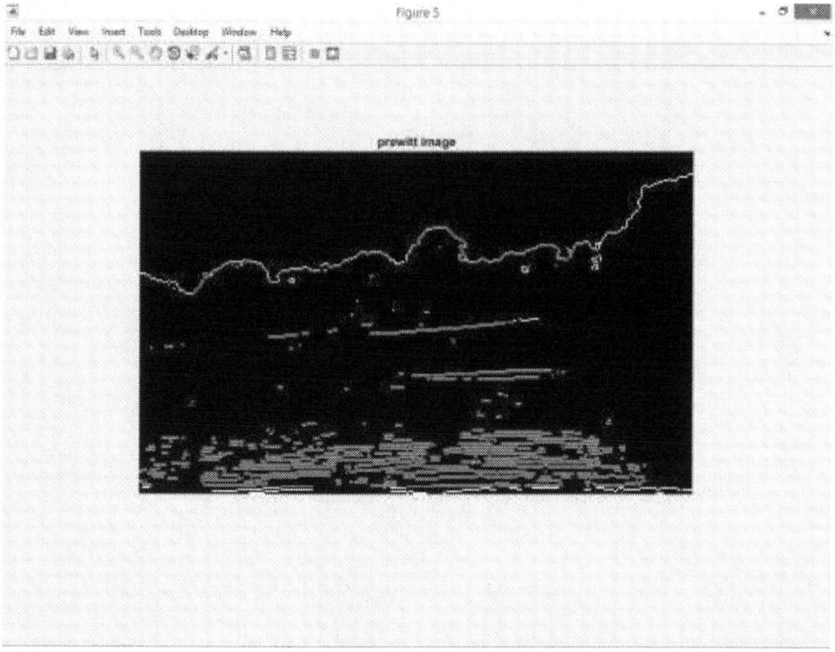


**Fig.5.** Prewitt Image

**Fig.6.** Log image

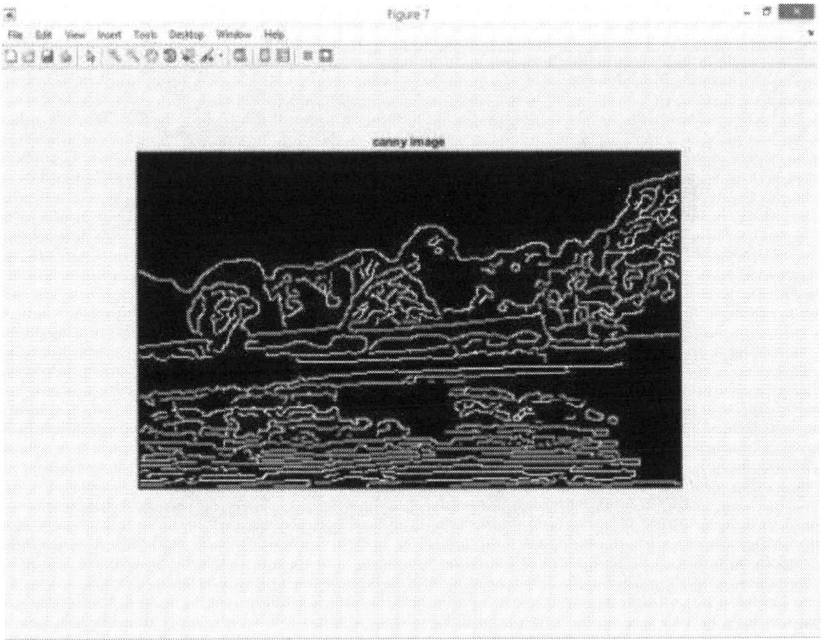


**Fig.7.** Canny Image

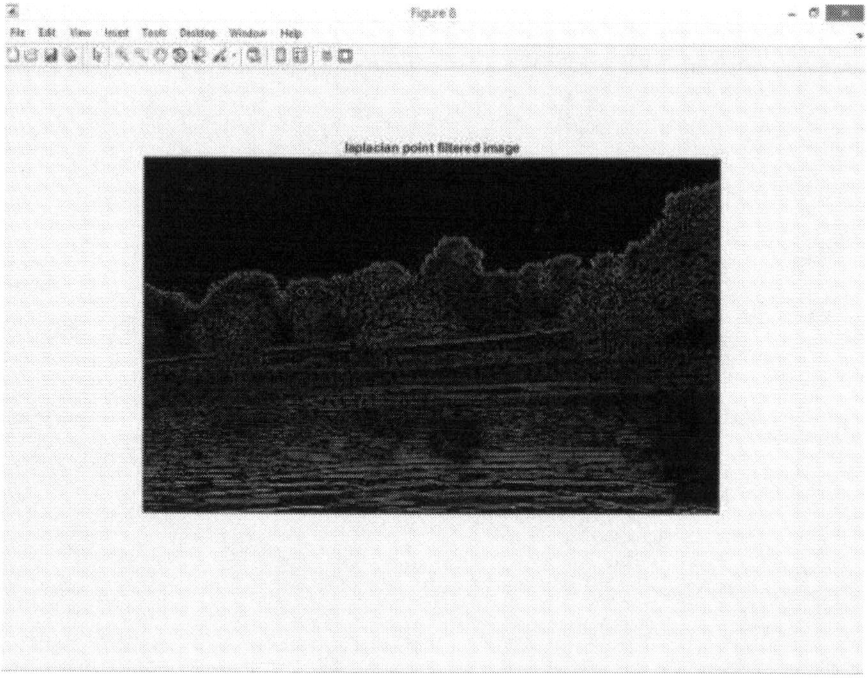


**Fig.8.** Laplacian Point Filtering Image

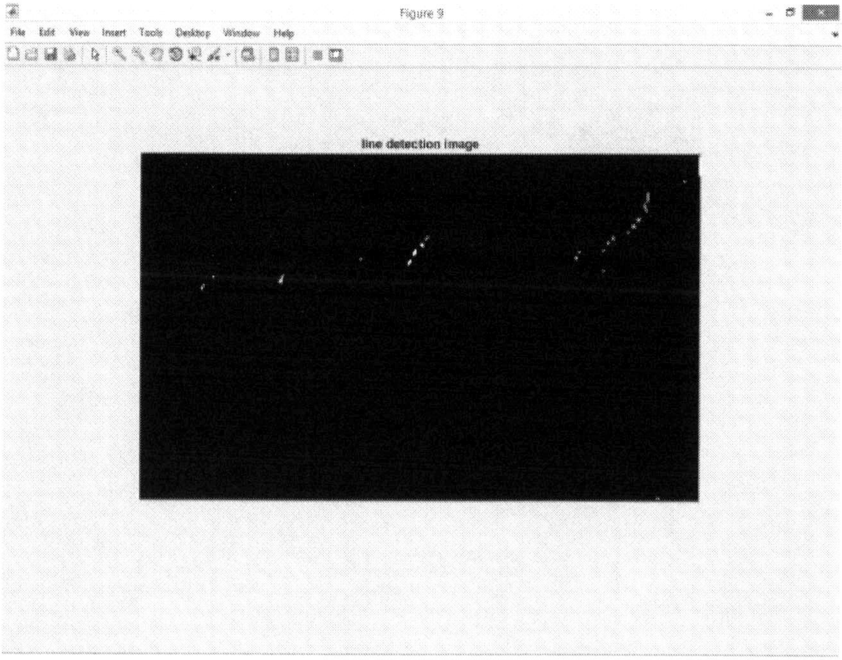


**Fig.9.** line detection Image

## APPLICATION

Real-world applications of image segmentation are:

1. Machine vision
2. Deep Learning
3. Medical imaging, including volume rendered images from CT (Computed Tomography) and MRI (Magnetic Resonance Imaging).
4. Measure tissue volumes
5. Surgery planning
6. Intra-surgery navigation
7. Locate tumors and pathologies
8. Virtual surgery simulation
9. Diagnosis, learning of anatomical structure
10. Pedestrian recognition
11. Object recognition
12. Face detection
13. Face recognition
14. Recognition Tasks
15. Fingerprint recognition
16. Iris recognition
17. Traffic controller schemes
18. Brake light detection
19. Video investigation
20. Find objects in satellite images like roads, forests, crops.

## Conclusion

Since edge detection is the first step in object boundary extraction and object recognition, it is significant to know the differences between different edge detection operators. from this section an attempt is made to review the edge detection methods which are based on discontinuity intensity levels. The relative presentation of various edge detection techniques is carried out with two images by using MATLAB. It have been experiential that that the Canny edge detector produces greater accuracy in detection of object edges with greater entropy, PSNR, MSE and  implementation time compared with Sobel, Roberts, Prewitt, Zero crossing and LOG.

# CHAPTER 3.

# INTENSITY TRANSFORMATION

## THEORETICAL CONCEPTS: INTRODUCTION

**What is Intensity Transformation?**

Intensity transformation is increase the contrast between certain Intensity values, most important application of intensity transformation is Enhance the low Quality image.

**Image Enhancement Techniques**

1. Spatial operates on Pixels
2. Frequency domain operates on Fourier transform of image

**Spatial Domain Methods**

- Spatial Domain Technique a operation (linear or non-linear) is performed on the pixels in the neighborhood of coordinate (x,y) in the input image F, giving enhanced image F'
- Neighborhood can be any shape but generally it is rectangular ( 3x3, 5x5, 9x9)

$$g(x,y) = T[f(x,y)]$$

## Grey Scale Manipulation

- Simplest form of window (1x1)
- Assume input gray scale values are in range [0, L-1] (in 8 bit images L = 256)
- $N^{th}$ root Transformation $S = c\,(r)^n$.

## Intensity Transformation function

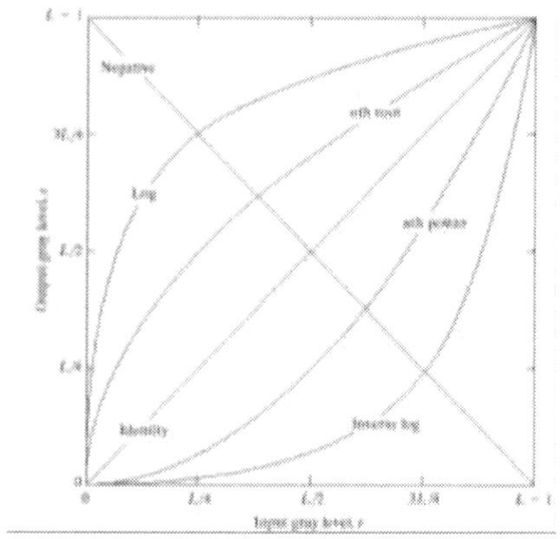

- **Linear:**

1. Negative
2. Identity

- **Logarithmic:**

1. Log
2. Inverse Log

- **Power-Law:**

1. *n*th power,
2. *n*th root.

**Negative Image**

$$S = (L - 1) - r$$

- L- Number of gray Level in image
- r- Pixel of input image

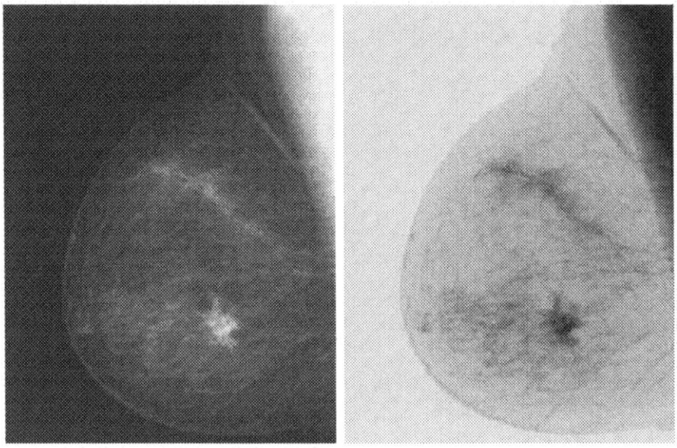

(Courtesy of G.E Medical system)

**Fig.1.** Original Mammogram image

**Fig.2.**Negative Image Obtained Using Negative Intensity transformation

**Log Transformation**

Compresses the dynamic range of images with big variations in pixel values

- $s = c \log(1+r)$
- c: constant

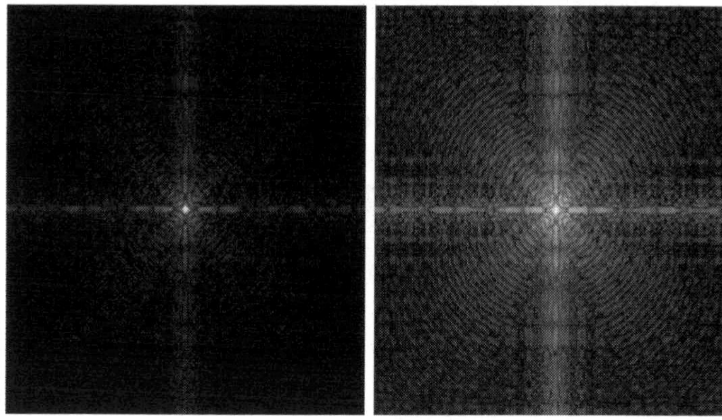

a) Fourier Spectrum b) Result of apply log transformation

**Power Law Transformation**

- $s = cr^{\gamma}$ for various values of $\gamma$ (c=1 in all case)
- C, $\gamma$ : positive constants
- Gamma correction

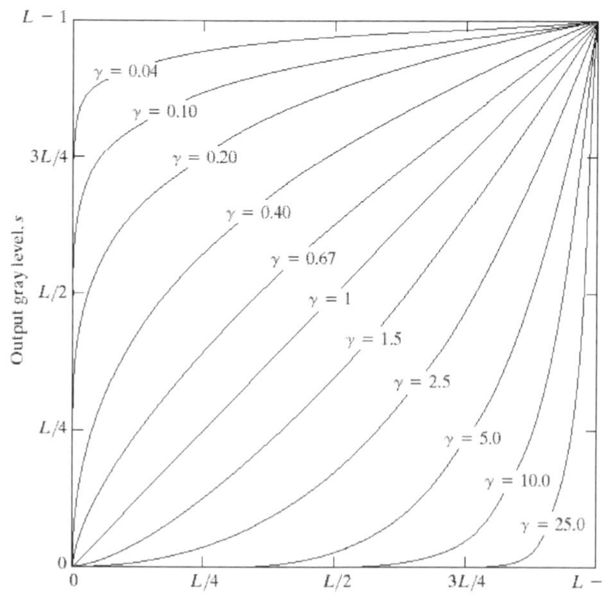

## Contrast Stretching

To increase the dynamic range of the gray levels in the image is being processed.

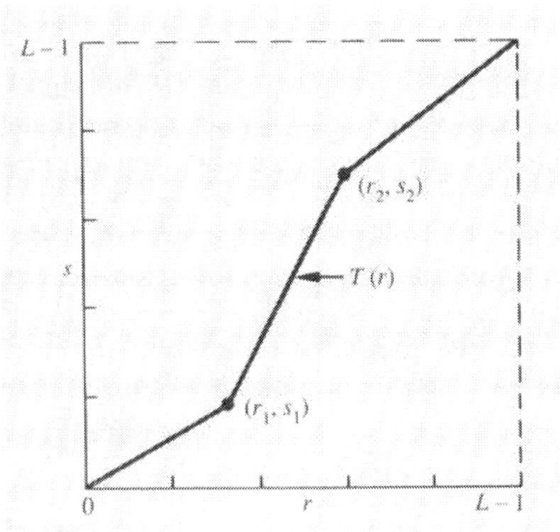


- The locations of **r1,** $s_1$ and **r2,** $s_2$ control the shape of the transformation function.
- If $r_1 = s_1$ and $r_2 = s_2$ the transformation is a linear function and produces no changes.
- If $r_1 = r_2$, $s_1 = 0$ and $s_2 = L-1$, the transformation becomes a thresholding function that creates a binary image.
- Intermediate values of $r_1$, $s_1$ and $r_2$, **s2** produce various degrees of spread in the gray levels of the output image, thus affecting its contrast.
- Commonly, $r_1 \leq r_2$ and $s_1 \leq s_2$ is assumed.

## Histogram Processing

The histogram of a digital image by gray levels from **0** to **L-1** is a discrete function **$h(r_k)=n_k$**, anywhere:

a) **$r_k$** is the **kth** gray level
b) **$n_k$** is the # pixels in the image by that gray level
c) **n** is the total number of pixels in the image
d) k = 0, 1, 2, …, L-1
e) Normalized histogram: **$p(r_k)=n_k/n$**
f) sum of all constituents = 1

## Histogram Equalization

$$s_k = T(r_k) = \sum_{j=0}^{k} \frac{n_j}{n} = \sum_{j=0}^{k} p_r(r_j)$$

Histogram equalization results are alike to contrast stretching however offer the advantage of full automation, since HE automatically determines a transformation function to yield a new image with a uniform histogram.

**Histogram Matching (or Specification)**

- Histogram equalization does not allow collaborating image enhancement and generates only one result: an approximation to a constant histogram.

- Sometimes however, we need to be able to specify particular histogram forms capable of highlighting certain gray-level ranges.

**Frequency Domain Methods**

- We simply compute the Fourier transform of the image to be enhanced, multiply the result by a filter and take the reverse transform to produce the enhanced image.
- Low pass filtering involves the rejection of the high frequency components in the image. It outcomes in blurring of the image

## Practical approach:

## MATLAB program Image Intensity Transformation

```
clc;

clear all;

close all;

%Read Input Image

a=imread('C:\Users\natheem\Desktop\images\mri.jpg');

subplot(2,2,1);

imshow(a);

title('original image');



%negative image

b=255-a;

subplot(2,2,2);

imshow(b);
```

```
title('negative image');


%log transform

l=255;

d=l/log10(1+l);

e=d*log10(1+double(a));

f=uint8(e);

subplot(2,2,3);

imshow(f);

title('log transform');


%power law transform

gamma=1.1;

g=double(a).^gamma;

subplot(2,2,4);

imshow(uint8(g));

title('power law transform');
```

# RESULT

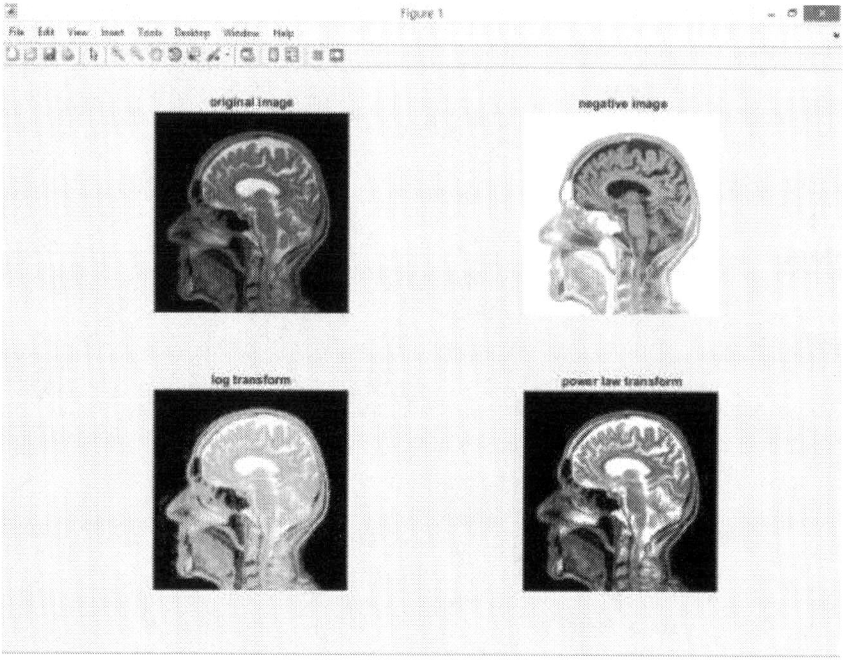


**Fig.2.1** Intensity Transformation using Subplots

## MATLAB PROGRAM USING INDIVIDUAL FIGURE

```
clc;

clear all;

close all;


%Read Input Image

a=imread('C:\Users\natheem\Desktop\images\mri.jpg');

figure(1);

imshow(a);

title('original image');


%negative image

b=255-a;

figure(2);

imshow(b);

title('negative image');


%log transform

l=255;

d=l/log10(1+l);
```

```
e=d*log10(1+double(a));

f=uint8(e);

figure(3);

imshow(f);

title('log transform');


%power law transform

gamma=1.1;

g=double(a).^gamma;

figure(4);

imshow(uint8(g));

title('power law transform');
```

**RESULT**

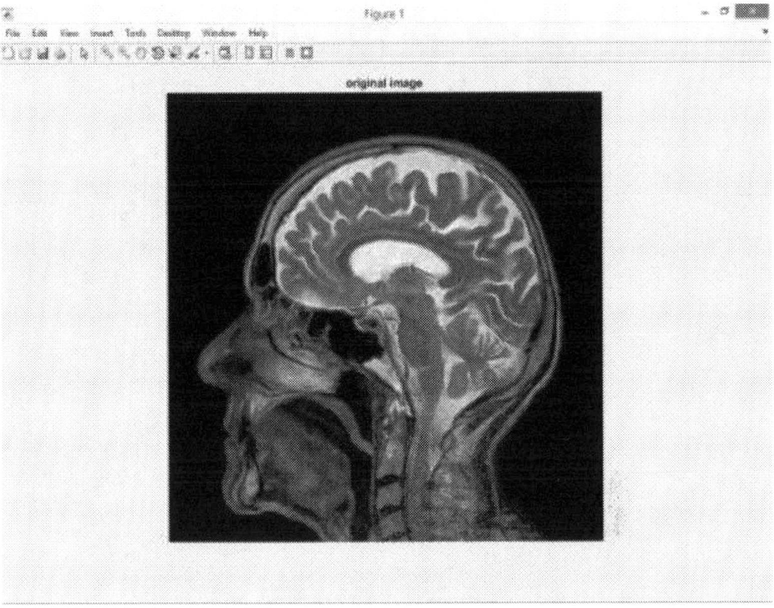


**Fig.2.1.1**.Original Image

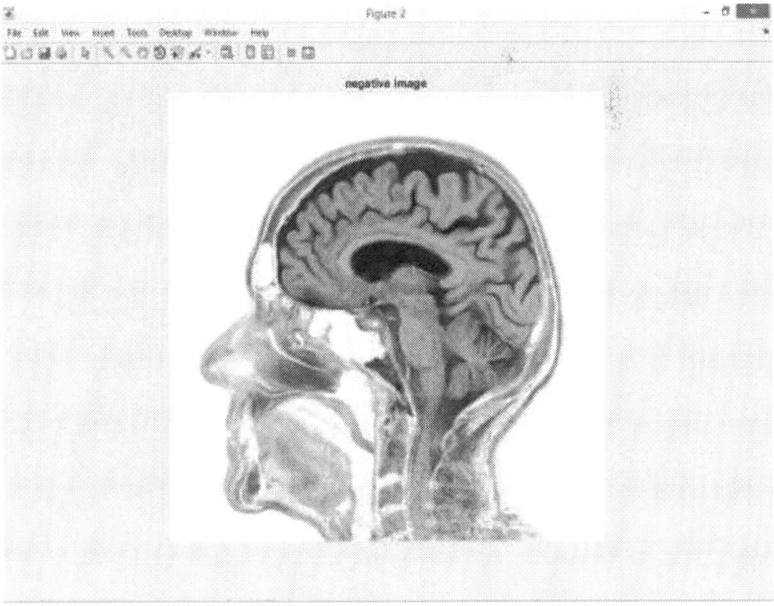


**Fig.2.1.2**.Negative Image

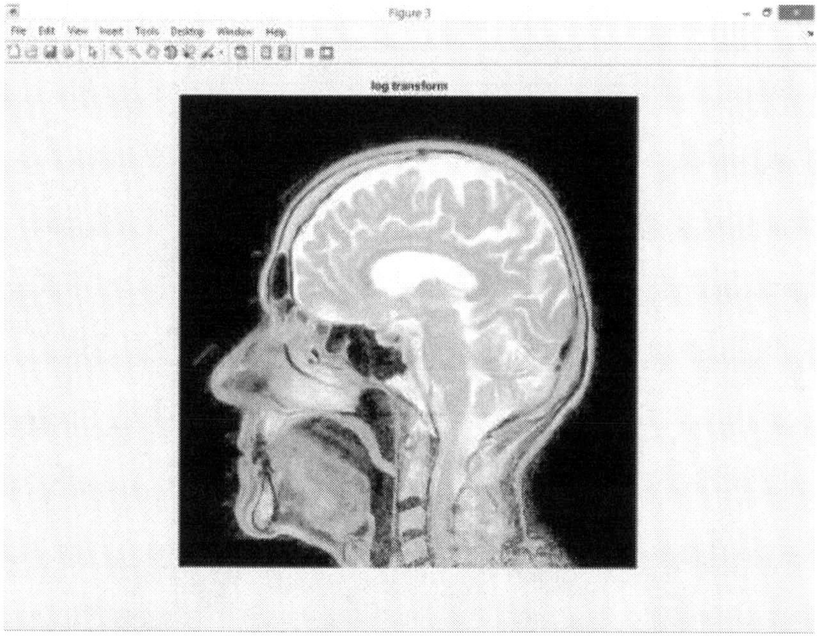


**Fig.2.1.3**.Log Transformation

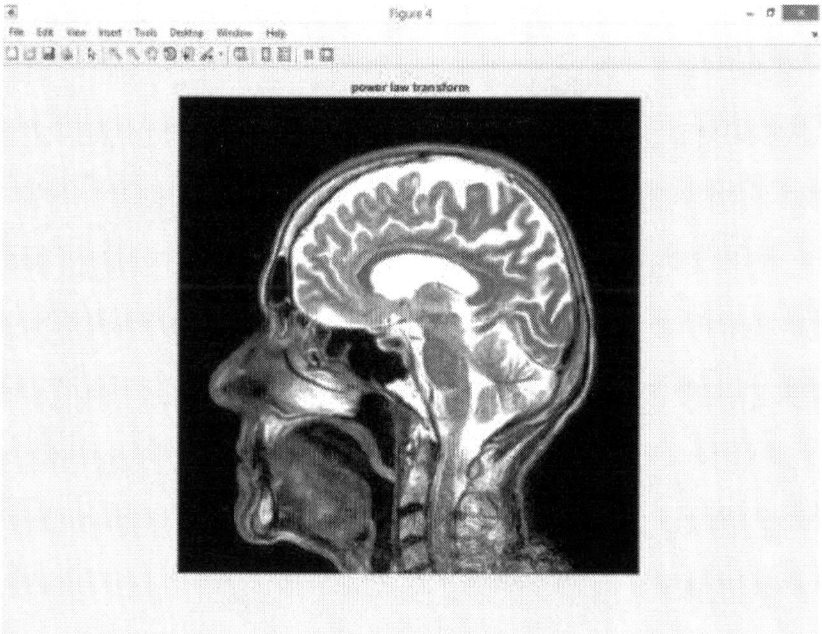


**Fig.2.1.4.** Power Law transformation

# OUTPUT FOR X-RAY IMAGE USING SUBPLOT

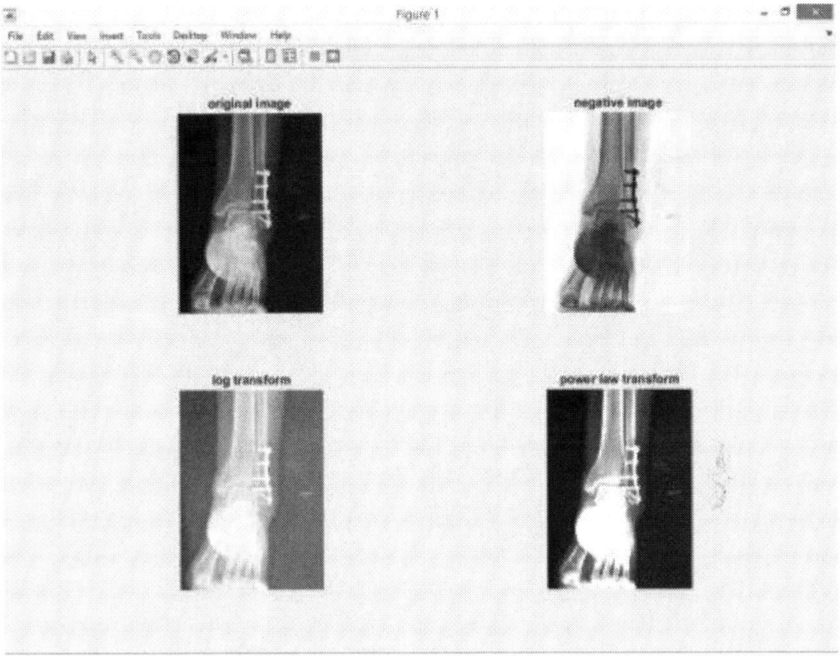


a) Original Image
b) Negative Image
c) Log transformation
d) Power law transformation

**OUTPUT FOR X-RAY IMAGE USING SEPARATE FIGURE**

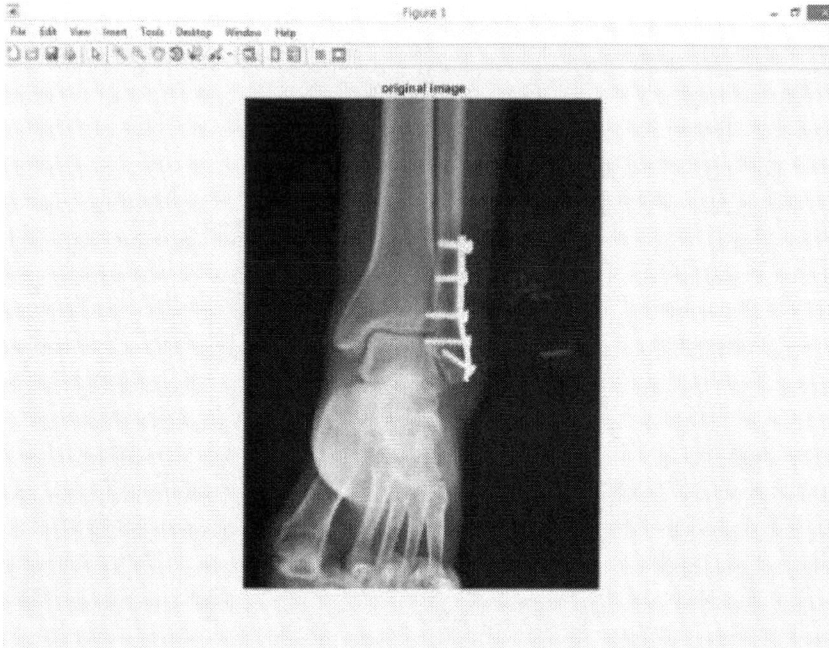


Fig.2.2.1 Original image

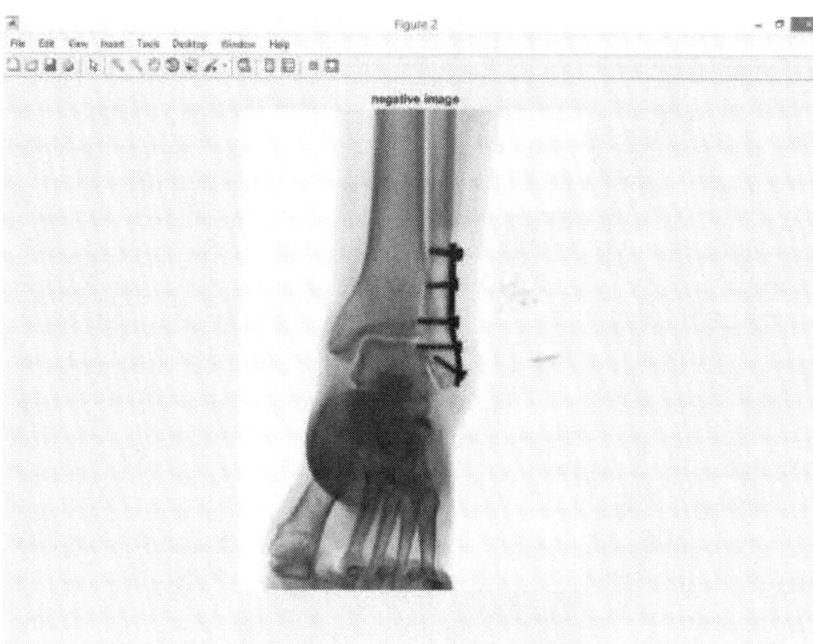


Fig.2.2.2 Negative Image

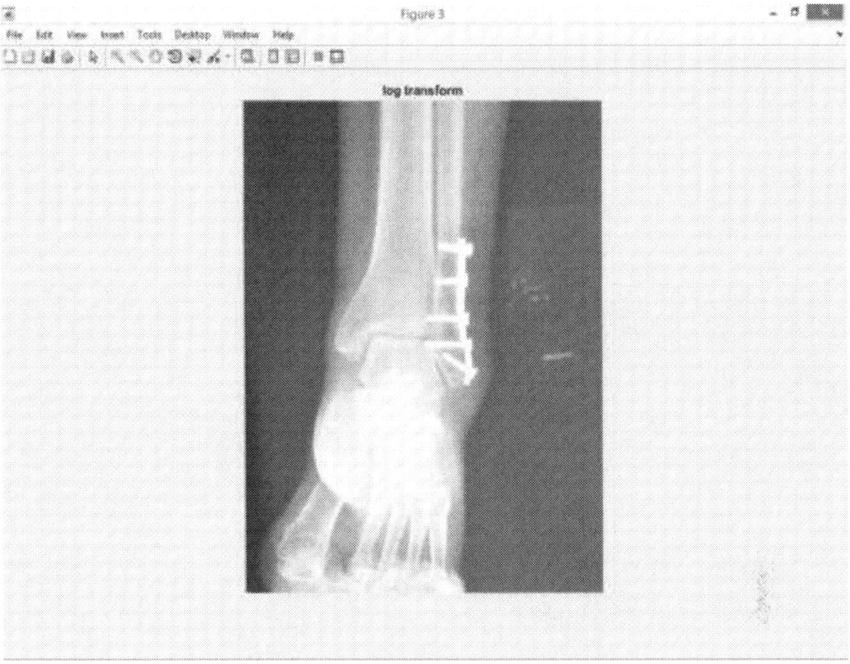


Fig.2.2.3 Log Transformation

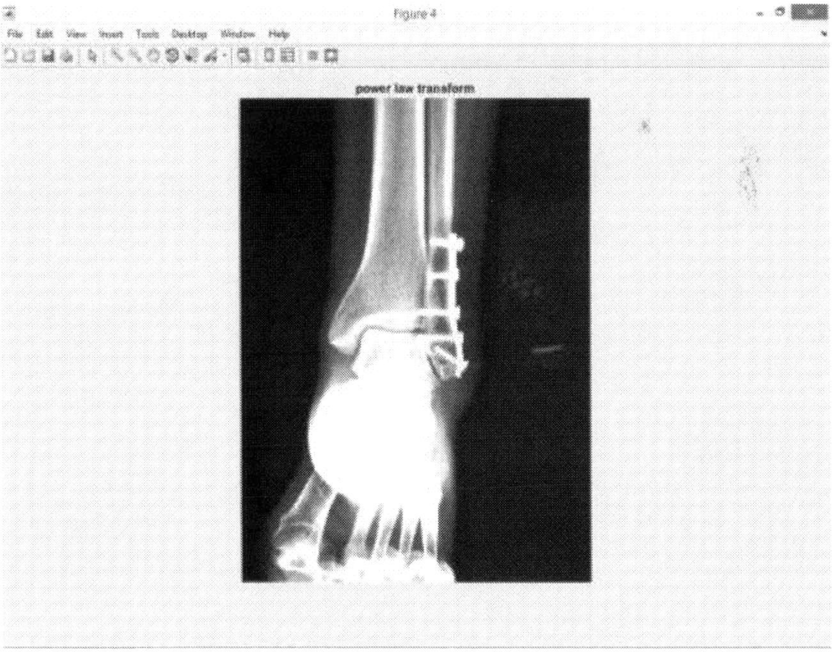


Fig.2.2.4 Power law Transformation

# CHAPTER 4.

## HISTOGRAM EQUALIZATION

### INTRODUCTION:

This application note defines a technique of Digital imaging processing which allows medical images to have better contrast. This is achieved via the histogram of the image, making use of a technique that allows the places with minimal contrast to improvement increasing contrast by circulation out the most regular intensity values. For example, in digital x-rays in what kind of colors achieved are a palette of whites and blacks, unlike types of colors give the physician an idea of the type of density that he or she is perceiving. Therefore white components are most likely to indicate bone or water and black structures mean air. Whenever pathologies are existing in an image, attempting to define the region of the lesion or object of interest may be a challenge, because a variety of structures are usually layered one over the other. like in the case of the chest the heart, lungs, and blood vessels are so near with each other that contrast is critical for accomplishing an accurate detection of problems.

## Digital Image

A digital image is a binary symbol of a 2D image. The digital exemplification is an array of picture elements called pixels. Each of these pixels has a numerical value which in homochromatic images represents a grey level

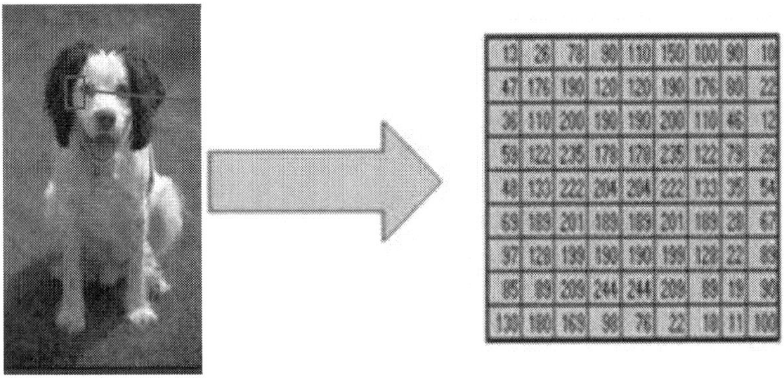

## Histogram of an image

Histogram is the approximation of the probability distribution of a particular type of data. An image histogram is a type of histogram which offers a graphical representation of the tonal distribution of the gray values in a digital image. By viewing the image's histogram, we can analyze the frequency of appearance of the different gray levels contained in the image. In we can see an image and its histogram.

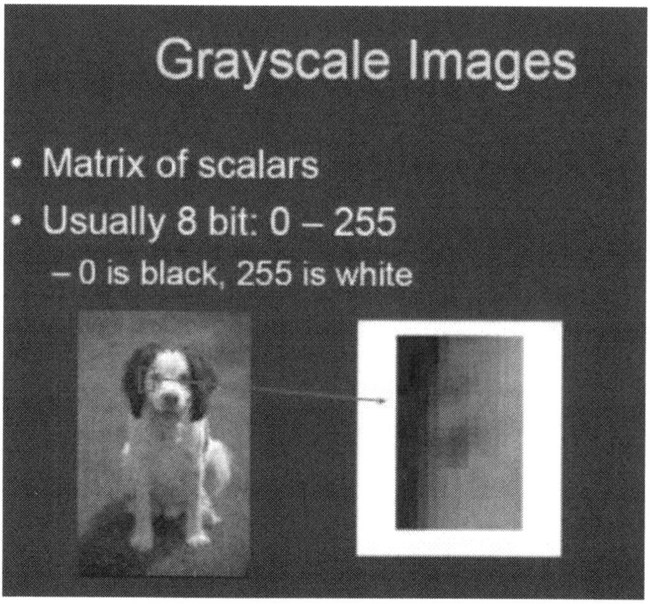


The histogram displays us that the image contains only a fraction of the entire range of gray levels. In this case there are 256 gray levels and the image only has values Between 50 to 100. Therefore this image has low contrast.

**What is a good Histogram?**

A good histogram is that which covers all the expected values in the gray scale used. This type of histogram proposes that the image has good contrast and that particulars in the image may be observed more easily.

## Methods for histogram equalization

- Histogram expansion
- Local area histogram equalization (LAHE)
- Cumulative histogram equalization
- Par sectioning
- Odd sectioning

**Table 1. Methods for histogram equalization**

| Method | Advantage | Disadvantage |
|---|---|---|
| Histogram expansion | Simple and enhance contrasts of an image. | If there are gray values that are physically far apart from each other in the image, then this method fails. |
| LAHE | Offers an excellent enhancement of image contrast. | Computationally very slow, requires a high number of operations per pixel. |
| Cumulative histogram equalization | Has good performance in histogram equalization. | Requires a few more operations because it is necessary to create the cumulative histogram. |
| Par sectioning | Easy to implement. | Better suited to hardware implementation. |
| Odd sectioning | Offers good image contrast. | Has problems with histograms which cover almost the full gray scale. |

### Histogram Processing

The histogram of a digital image with gray levels from **0** to **L-1** is a discrete function **$h(r_k)=n_k$**, wherever:

a) **$r_k$** is the **kth** gray level
b) **$n_k$** is the # pixels in the image with that gray level
c) **n** is the total number of pixels in the image
d) k = 0, 1, 2, …, L-1
e) Normalized histogram: **$p(r_k)=n_k/n$**
f) sum of all constituents = 1

### Histogram Equalization

$$s_k = T(r_k) = \sum_{j=0}^{k} \frac{n_j}{n} = \sum_{j=0}^{k} p_r(r_j)$$

Histogram equalization output are alike to contrast stretching however offer the advantage of full automation, meanwhile HE automatically determines a transformation function to produce a new image with a uniform histogram.

Fig.1 Dark Image vs High contrast histogram image

Fig.2. Histogram Equalized image

## Histogram Matching (or Specification)

- Histogram equalization does not allow cooperating image enhancement and makes only one result: an approximation to a constant histogram.

- Sometimes still, we need to be able to specify particular histogram forms capable of highlighting certain gray-level ranges.

**FLOW CHART**

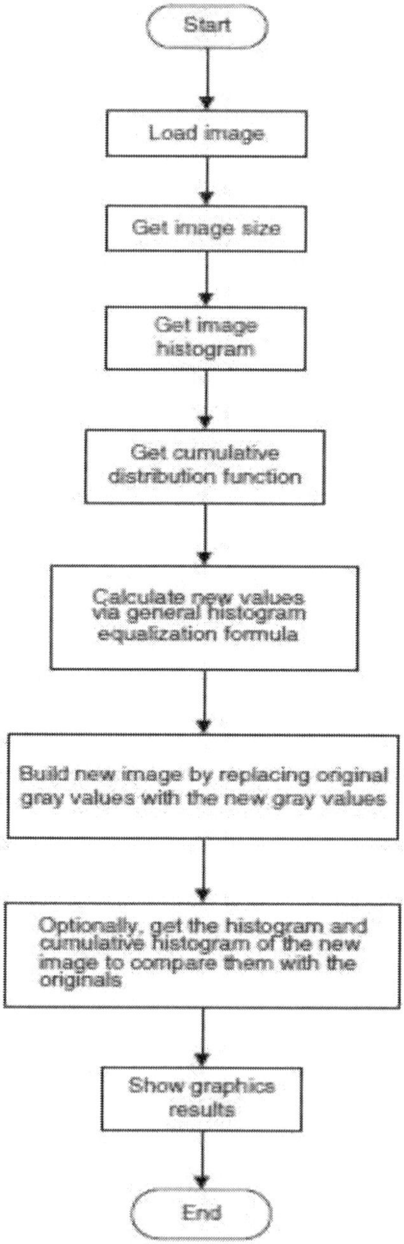
Start
Load image
Get image size
Get image histogram
Get cumulative distribution function
Calculate new values via general histogram equalization formula
Build new image by replacing original gray values with the new gray values
Optionally, get the histogram and cumulative histogram of the new image to compare them with the originals
Show graphics results
End

# MATLAB Source Code for Histogram Equalization

```
clc;

clear all;

close all;


%Read an input image

a=imread('C:\Users\nadeem\Desktop\palace.png');


%histogram processing

subplot(3,2,1);

imshow(a);

title('original image');


%converting to gray

subplot(3,2,3);

b=rgb2gray(a);

imshow(b);

title('grayscale image');
```

```
%equalisation of image

subplot(3,2,4);

c=histeq(b);

imshow(c);

title('equalised image');


subplot(3,2,5);

imhist(b);

title('histogram of grayscale image');


subplot(3,2,6);

imhist(c);

title('histogram of equalised image');
```

# OUTPUT

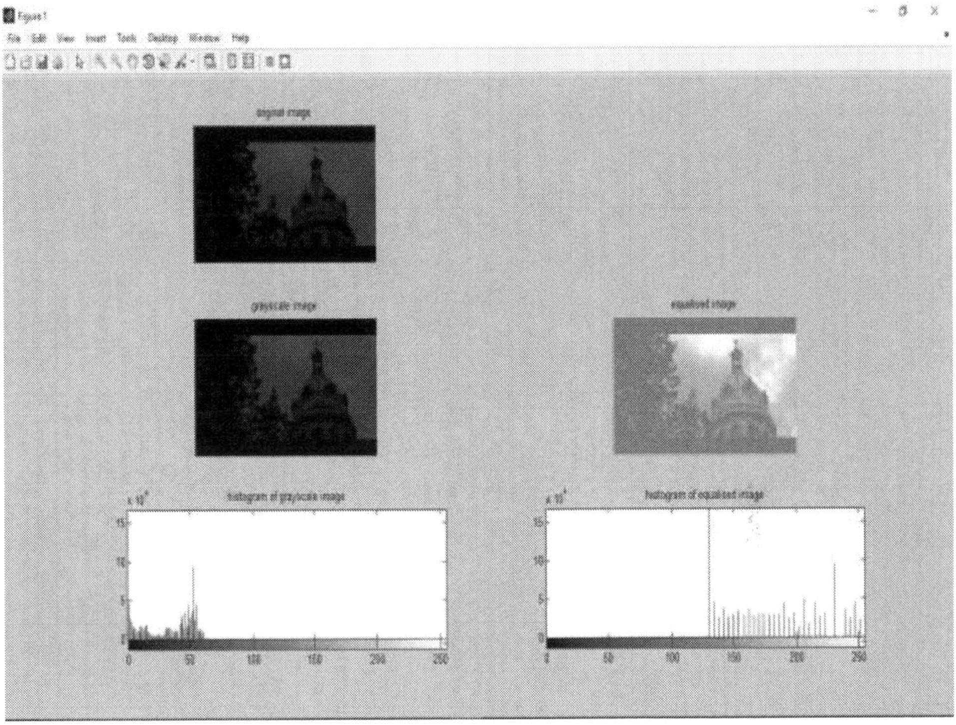


Fig.1. Histogram Equalization with subplots

**Fig.1** Original Image (Low contrast | Dark Image)

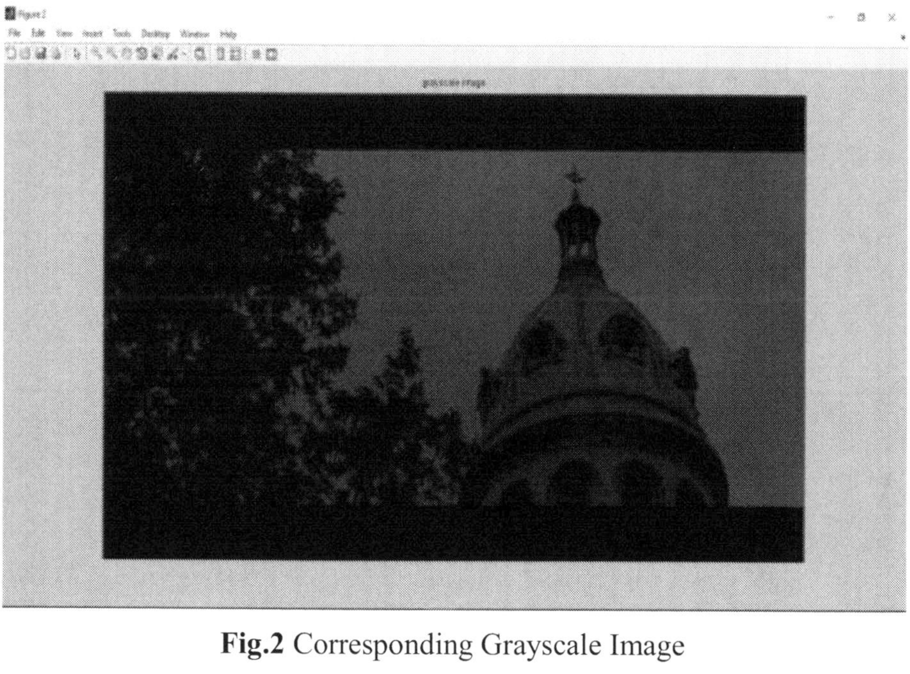

**Fig.2** Corresponding Grayscale Image

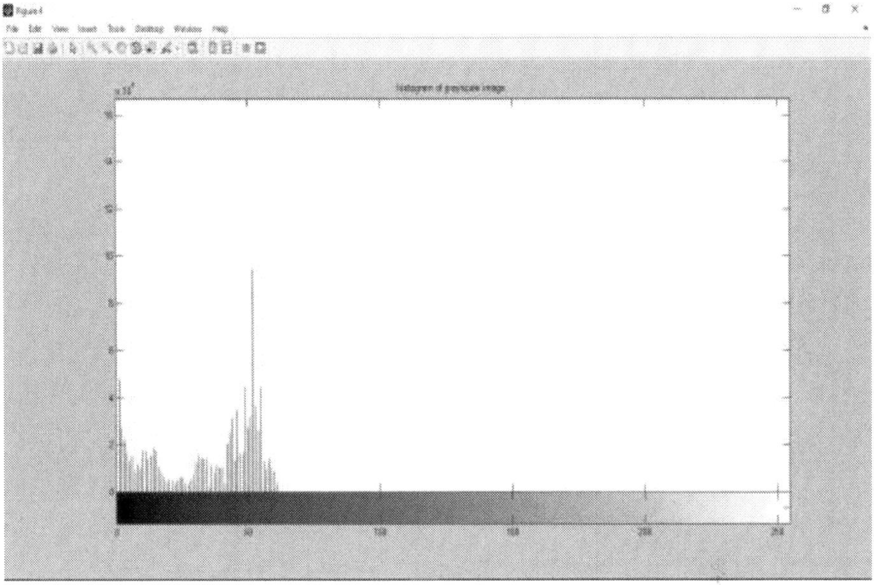

**Fig.4** Corresponding Histogram plot of grayscale image

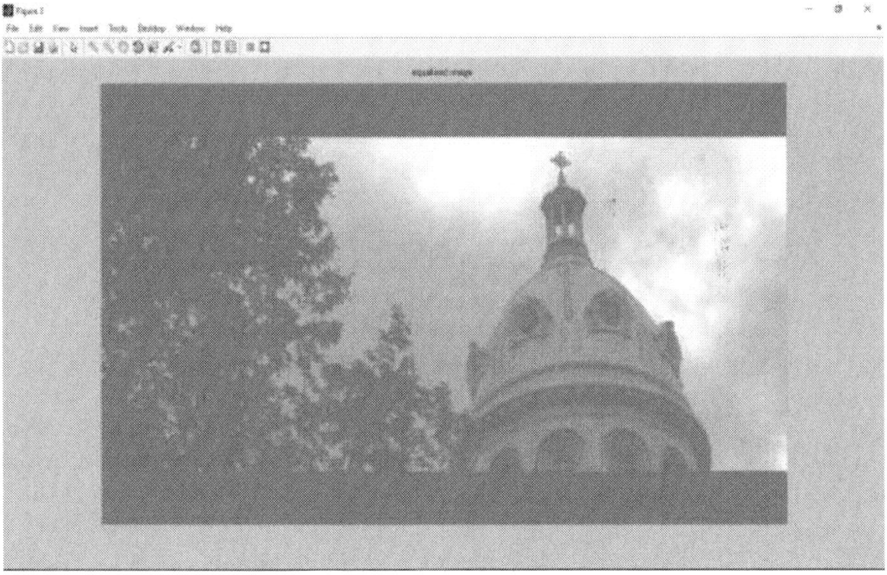

**Fig.3** Histogram Equalized image

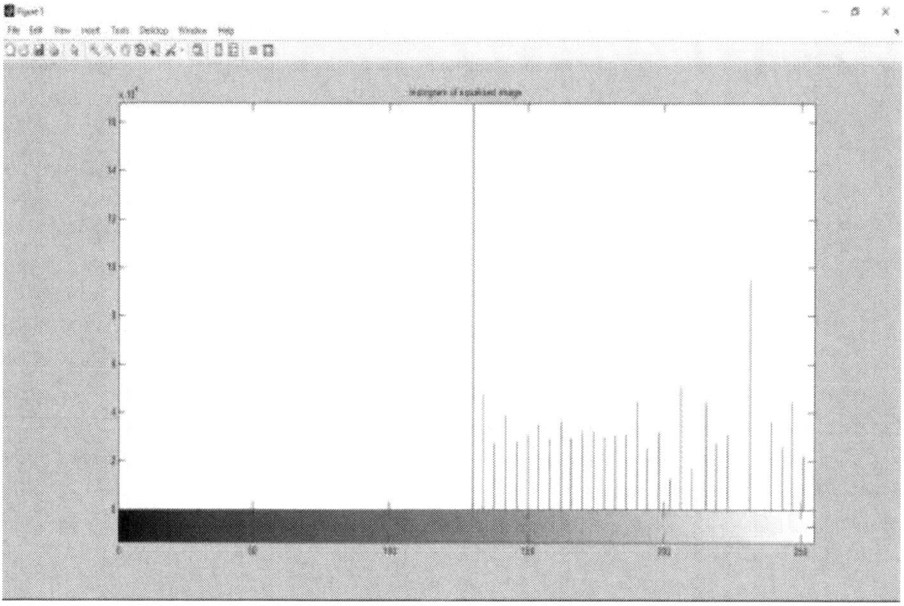

**Fig.5** Corresponding Histogram plot of Equalized image

# HISTOGRAM EQUALIZATION USING COLOR IMAGE

```
clc;

clear all;

close all;


%Read Color Image

a=imread('C:\Users\natheem\Desktop\images\monky.jpg');


%histogram processing

subplot(3,3,1);

imshow(a);

title('Original image');


%converting to gray

subplot(3,3,2);

b=rgb2gray(a);

imshow(b);

title('Grayscale image');


%equalisation of image
```

```
subplot(3,3,3);;

c=histeq(b);

imshow(c);

title('Equalised image');



subplot(3,3,5);

imhist(b);

title('Histogram of grayscale image');

 subplot(3,3,6);

imhist(c);

title('Histogram of equalised image');
```

**RESULT**

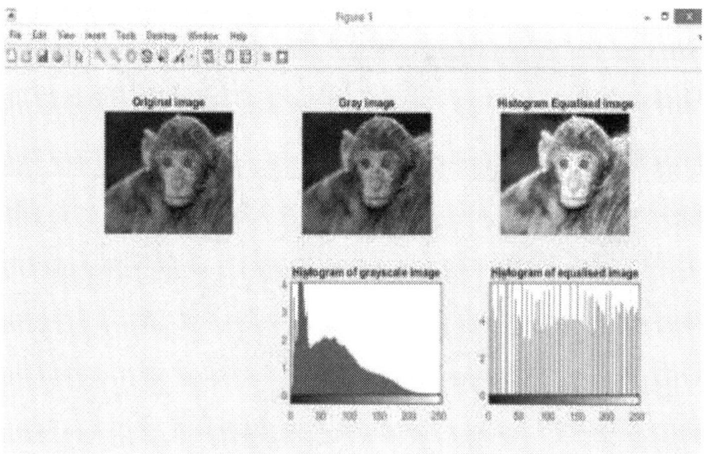

# OUTPUT WITH SEPARATE FIGURE

Fig.1. original Image

Fig.2.Grayscale image

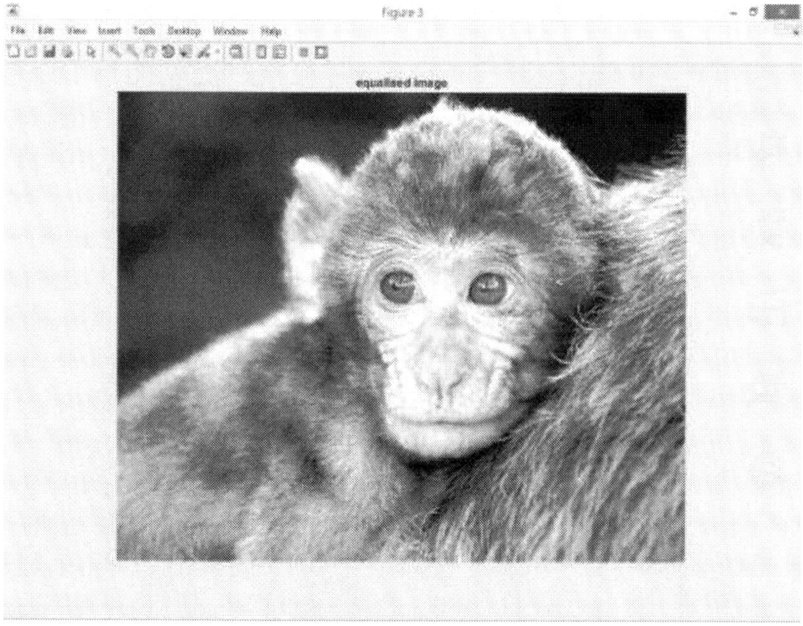


Fig.3.Histogram equalized image

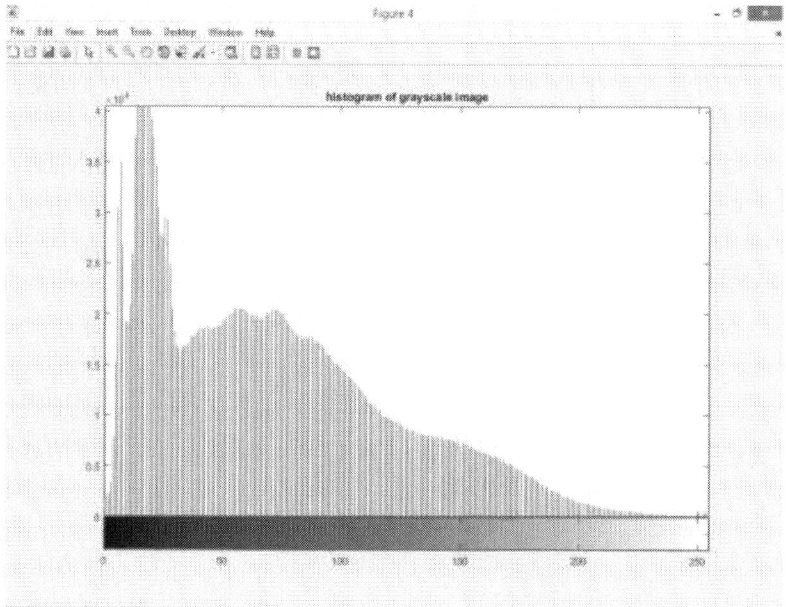


Fig.4.Histogram plot of grayscale image

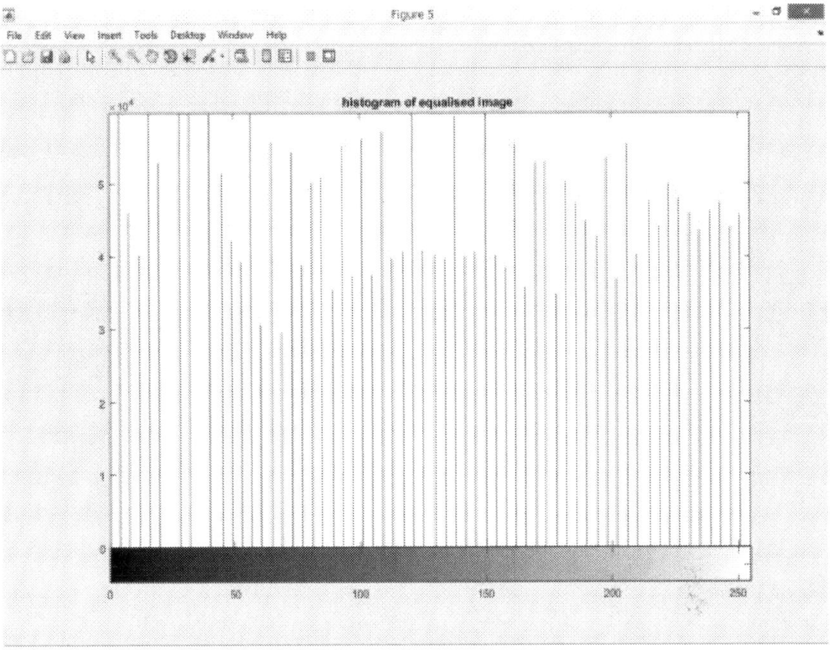


Fig.5. Histogram plot of Equalized image

## Conclusion

Histogram equalization is a direct image processing technique often used to achieve better quality images in black and white color balances in medical applications such as X-rays, MRIs, and CT scans. All these images require high definition and contrast of colors to determine the pathology that is being experiential and reach a diagnosis. Though, in some type of images histogram equalization can show noise hidden in the image after the processing is done.

# CHAPTER 5.

## SPATIAL INTENSITY RESOLUTION

### INTRODUCTION

Sampling is the principal factor Estimation of the spatial resolution of an image. Commonly spatial resolution is the smallest perceptible detail in an image, a widely used meaning of resolution is simply the smallest number of discernible line pairs per unit distance; for estimation 100 line pairs/mm.

Gray level resolution: This refers to the smallest visible change in gray level. The measurement of visible changes in gray level is a extremely subjective procedure.

We have significant discretion concerning the number of Samples used to generate a digital image. But this is not true for the amount of gray levels. Due to hardware restraints, the number of gray levels is usually an integer power of two. The most common value is 8 bits. It can vary depending on application. When an actual portion of physical resolution relating pixels and level of detail they resolution in the original scene are not necessary, it is not rare to refer to an L-level digital image of size  as consuming a spatial resolution of  pixels and a gray level resolution of L levels.

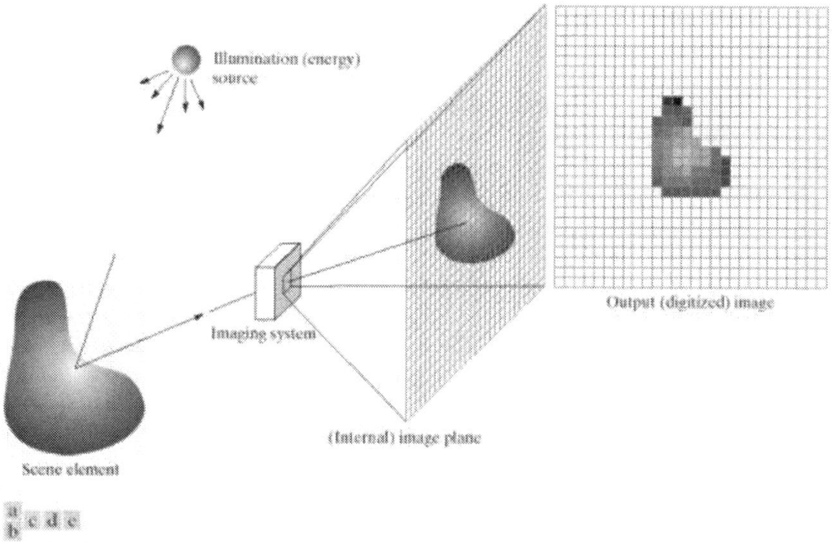


**FIGURE 2.15** An example of the digital image acquisition process. (a) Energy ("illumination") source. (b) An element of a scene. (c) Imaging system. (d) Projection of the scene onto the image plane. (e) Digitized image.

## Functional Representation of Images

- Two-D function f(x,y), (x,y) pixel position. Positive and bounded
- Written as f(x,y)=i(x,y)r(x,y), i(x,y) illumination from light source, r(x,y) reflectance (bounded between 0 and 1) based on material properties. E.g r(x,y)=0.01 for black velvet, r(x,y) = 0.93 for snow.
- Intensity of monochrome image f(x,y) is synonymous with *grey levels*. By convention grey level are from 0 to L-1.

•

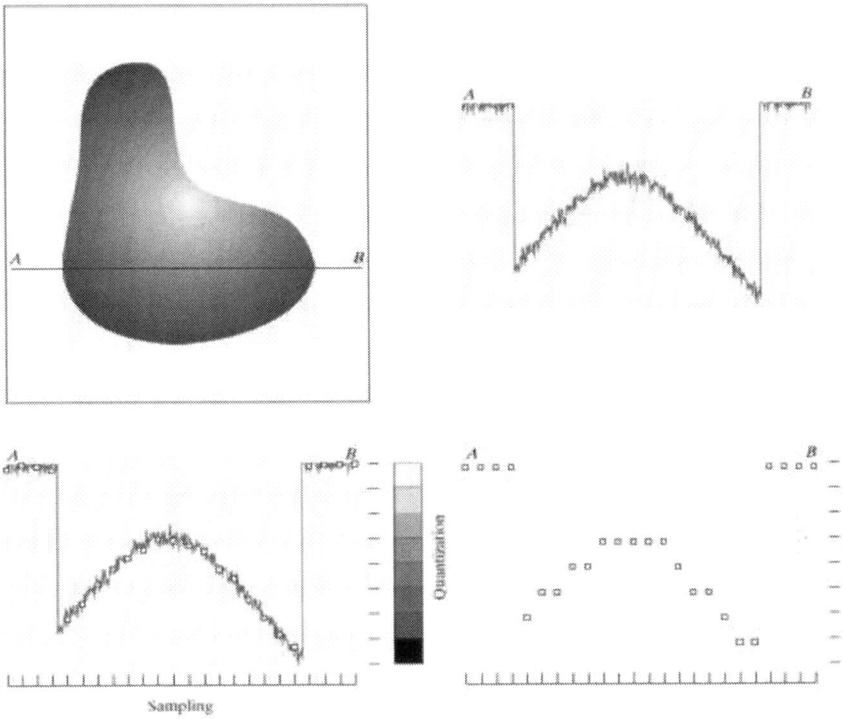


a b
c d

**FIGURE 2.16** Generating a digital image. (a) Continuous image. (b) A scan line from *A* to *B* in the continuous image, used to illustrate the concepts of sampling and quantization. (c) Sampling and quantization. (d) Digital scan line.

## Spatial and Gray Level Resolution

- *Spatial resolution* is the lowest level of detail discernable in an image. Number of line sets per millimeter, approximately 100 line pairs per millimeter.
- *Gray-level resolution* is the lowest discernable change in gray level. Very Subjective.

# Spatial resolution and intensity resolution

- Sampling is the principal factor defining the spatial resolution of an image, and quantization is the principal factor defining the intensity resolution
- Spatial resolution - number of rows and columns for example: 128 x128, 256 by 256, etc.; -->see Figs. 2.19 and 2.20
- Intensity resolution - number of gray levels for example: 8 bits, 16 bits, etc.; --->see Fig. 2.21

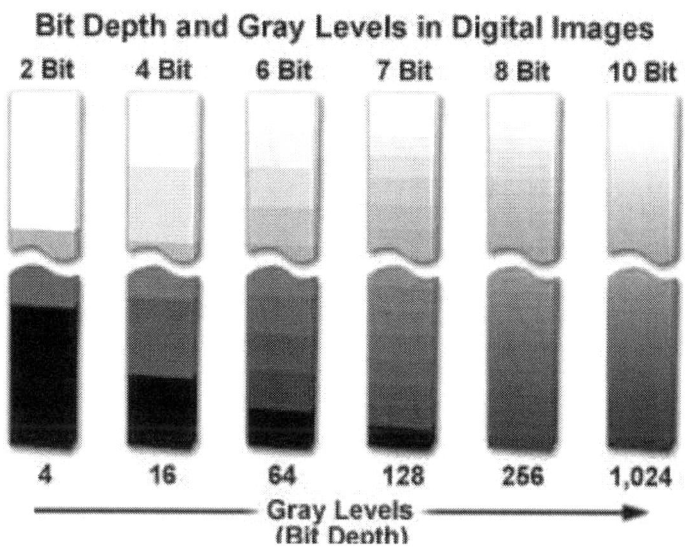

a b c
d e f

**FIGURE 2.20** (a) $1024 \times 1024$, 8-bit image. (b) $512 \times 512$ image resampled into $1024 \times 1024$ pixels by row and column duplication. (c) through (f) $256 \times 256$, $128 \times 128$, $64 \times 64$, and $32 \times 32$ images resampled into $1024 \times 1024$ pixels.

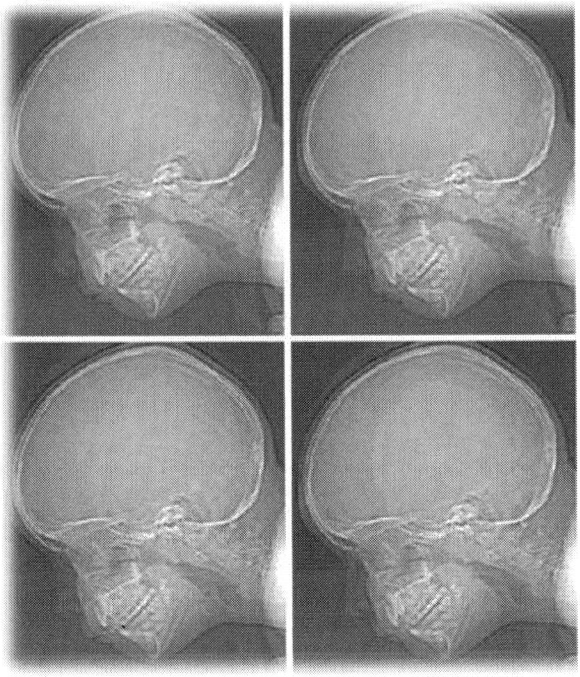

c d

**FIGURE 2.21** (a) $452 \times 374$, 256-level image. (b)–(d) Image displayed in 128, 64, and 32 gray levels, while keeping the spatial resolution constant.

Image Enhancement in Spatial Domain Find gray level transformation function T(r) to obtains (x,y) =T(f(x,y)) processed image from input image.

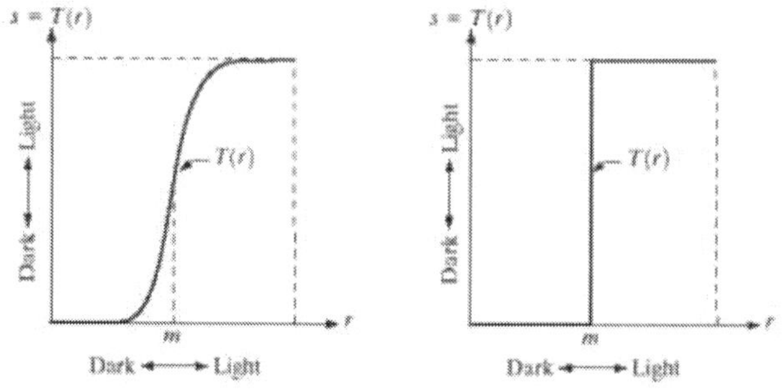


a b
**FIGURE 3.2** Gray-level transformation functions for contrast enhancement.

**REASONS**

1. Contrast enhancement
2. Image understanding
3. Visual improvement

**Picture Reference:**

Photos Reference from Digital Image Processing, Gonzalez and Woods, Copyright 2002

# MATLAB Source Code For Spatial Intensity Resolution

```
clc;
clear all;
close all;
a=imread('C:\Users\natheem\Desktop\images\satelite.jpg');
subplot(3,2,1);
imshow(a);
title('original image');
%
subplot(3,2,2);
imshow(grayslice(a,128),gray(128));
title('128 graylevel image');
%
subplot(3,2,3);
imshow(grayslice(a,64),gray(64));
title('64 graylevel image');
%
subplot(3,2,4);
imshow(grayslice(a,32),gray(32));
```

```
title('32 graylevel image');

%

subplot(3,2,5);

imshow(grayslice(a,16),gray(16));

title('16 graylevel image');

%

subplot(3,2,6);

imshow(grayslice(a,8),gray(8));

title('8 graylevel image');
```

**Result**

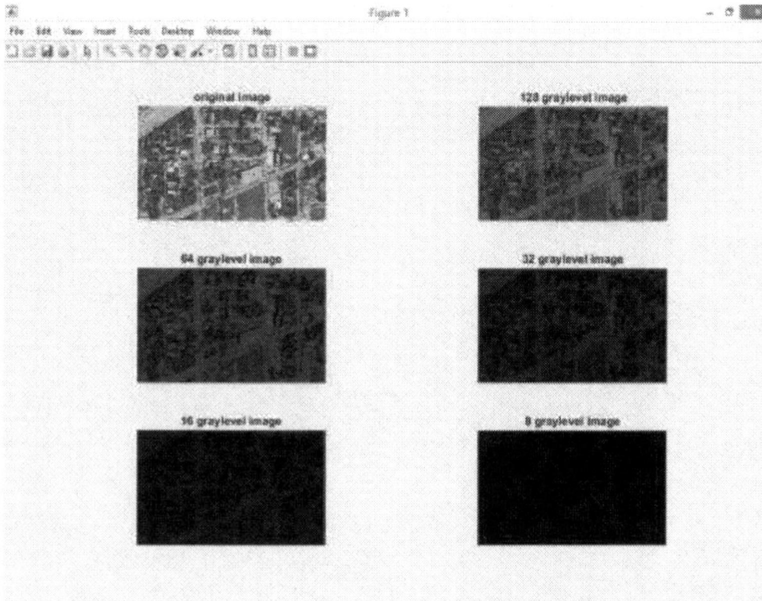

## MATLAB PROGRAM USING INDIVIDUAL FIGURE

```
clc;
clear all;
close all;
a=imread('C:\Users\natheem\Desktop\images\satelite.jpg');
figure(1);
imshow(a);
title('original image');
 %128 graylevel image
figure(2);
imshow(grayslice(a,128),gray(128));
title('128 graylevel image');

%64 graylevel image
figure(3);
imshow(grayslice(a,64),gray(64));
title('64 graylevel image');

%32 graylevel image
figure(4);
```

```
imshow(grayslice(a,32),gray(32));

title('32 graylevel image');


%16 graylevel imag

figure(5);

imshow(grayslice(a,16),gray(16));

title('16 graylevel image');


%8 graylevel image

figure(6);

imshow(grayslice(a,8),gray(8));

title('8 graylevel image');
```

**Output**

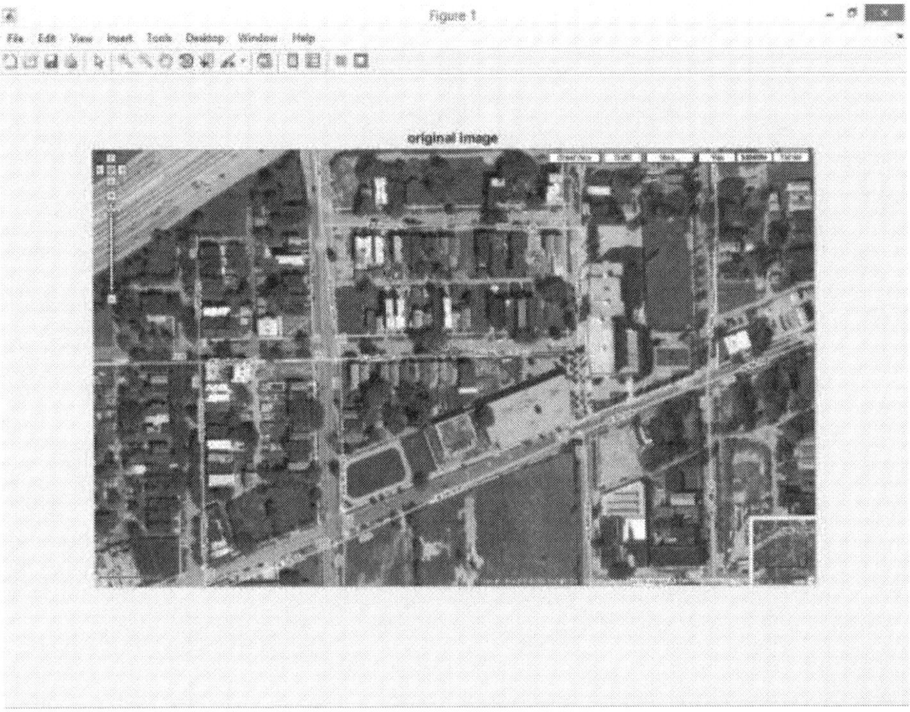
Figure 1
File Edit View Insert Tools Desktop Window Help
original image

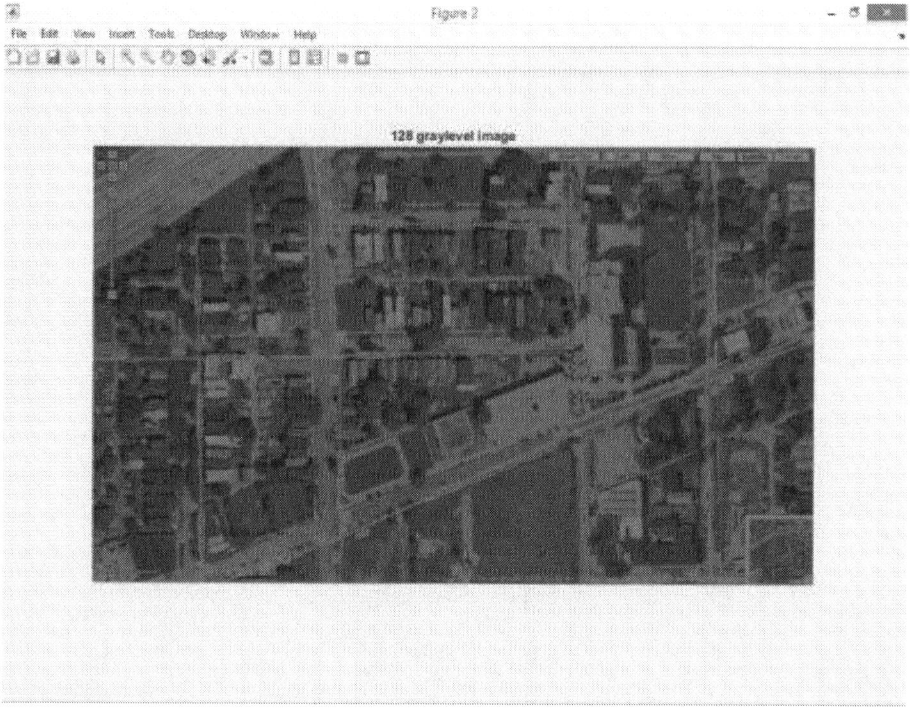
Figure 2
File Edit View Insert Tools Desktop Window Help
128 graylevel image

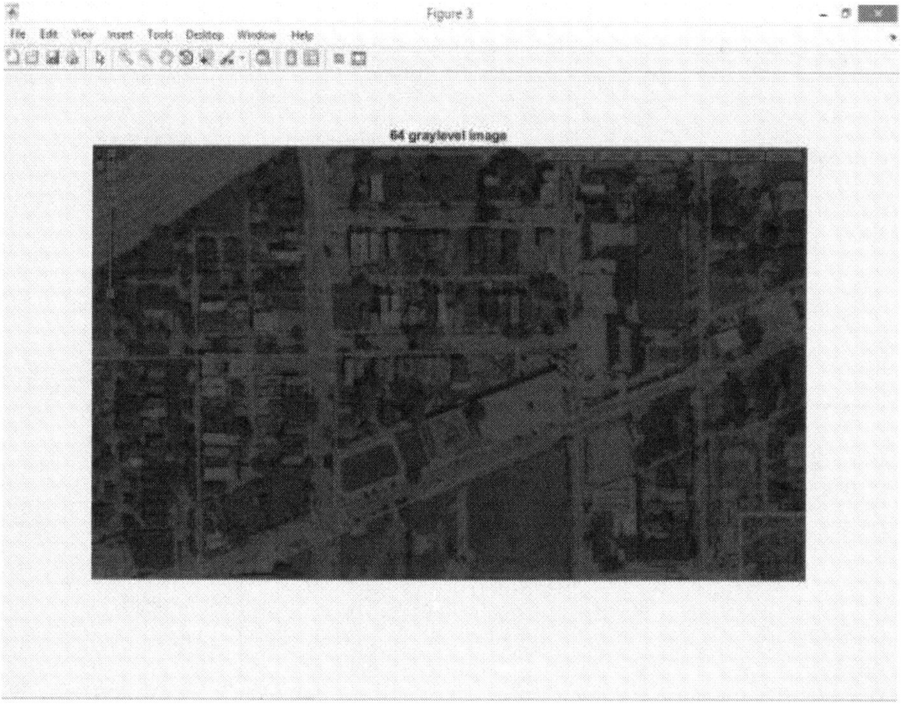
Figure 3
File Edit View Insert Tools Desktop Window Help
64 graylevel image

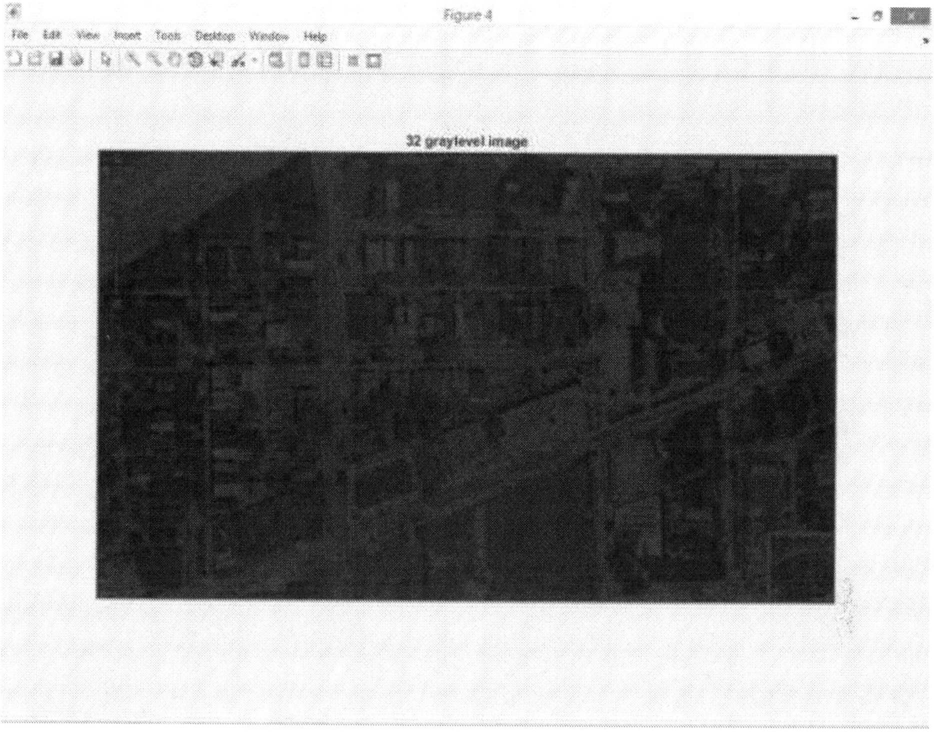
Figure 4
File Edit View Insert Tools Desktop Window Help
32 graylevel image

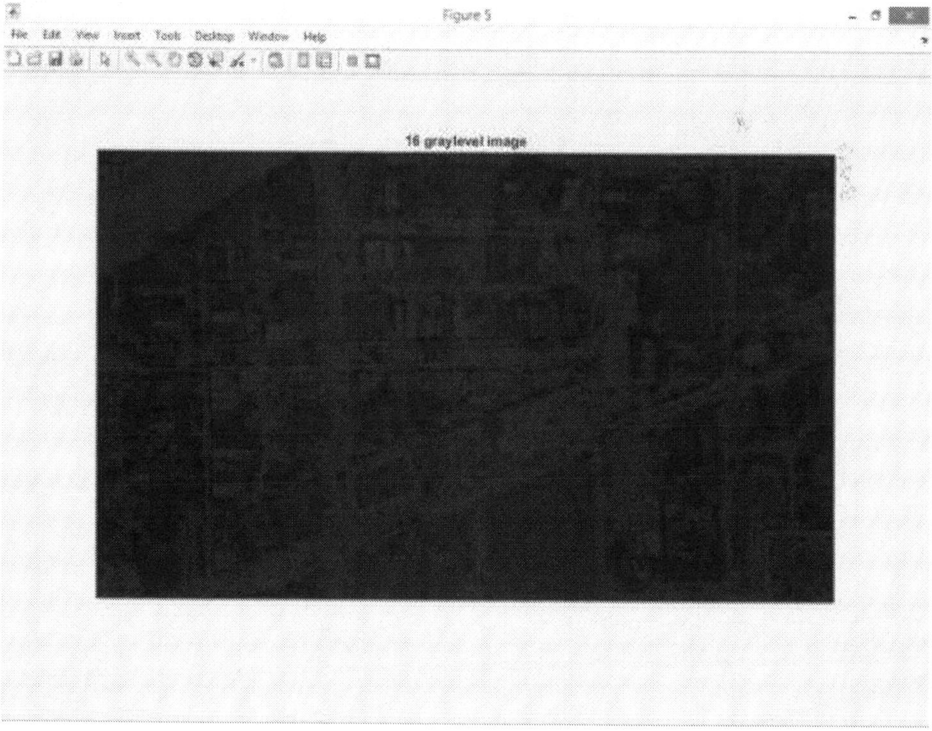
Figure 5
File Edit View Insert Tools Desktop Window Help
16 graylevel image

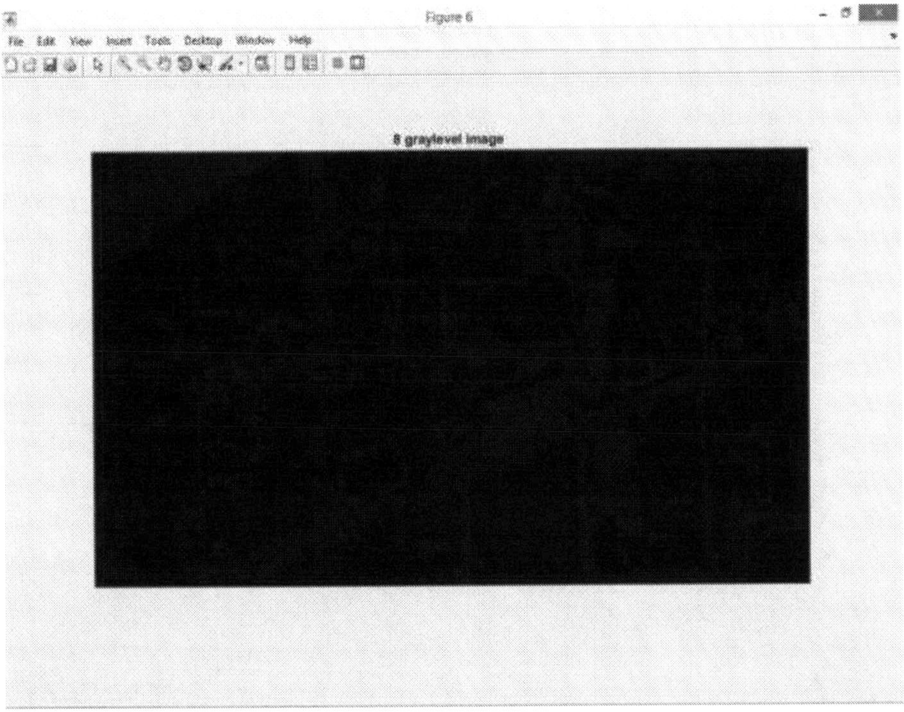
Figure 6
File Edit View Insert Tools Desktop Window Help
8 graylevel image

# CHAPTER 6.

# ENHANCEMENT IN SPATIAL FILTER

## Introduction

- Filter term in "Digital image processing" is stated to the subimage, filtering is a technique for adapting or enhancing an image.
- There are others term to call subimage such as kernel, mask, template, or window
- The value in a filter subimage are stated as coefficients, rather than pixels.

## Basics of Spatial Filtering

Spatial filtering term is the filtering operations that are performed directly on the pixels of an image, Spatial domain operation or filtering (the processed value for the present pixel processed value for the present pixel be contingent on both itself and nearby pixels). Henceforth Filtering is a region operation, the value of any assumed pixel in the output image is determined by applying some procedure to the values of the pixels in the neighborhood of the consistent input pixel. A pixel's area is some set of pixels, defined by their positions relative to that pixel. The concept of filtering has its roots in the use of the Fourier transform for signal processing in the so-called frequency domain.

## Mechanics of spatial filtering

- The process contains simply of moving the filter mask from point to point in an image.
- At each point (x,y) the response of the filter at that point is calculated using a predefined relationship

## Linear spatial filtering

Generally, linear filtering of an image f of size MxN with a filter mask of size mxn is given by the expression

$$g(x,y)=\sum_{s=-a}^{a}\sum_{t=-b}^{b}w(s,t)f(x+s,y+t)$$

- The result is the sum of products of the mask coefficients with the corresponding pixels directly under the mask
- The coefficient w(0,0) coincides with image value f(x,y), indicating that the mask is centered at (x,y) when the computation of sum of products takes place.

- For a mask of size mxn, we assume that m-2a+1 and n=2b+1, where a and b are nonnegative integer. Then m and n are odd.

- The process of linear filtering similar to a frequency domain concept called "*convolution*"

**Nonlinear spatial filtering**

- Nonlinear spatial filters also operate on neighborhoods, and the mechanism of sliding a mask previous an image are the same as was just outlined.
- The filtering operation is based conditionally on the values of the pixels in the neighborhood under consideration

**Smoothing Spatial Filters**

- Smoothing filters are used for blurring and for noise reduction.
- Blurring is used in preprocessing stages, such as removal of small details from an image prior to object extraction, and bridging of small gaps in lines or curves
- Noise reduction can be accomplished by blurring

**Type of smoothing filtering**

There are two types of smoothing spatial filters

1. Smoothing Linear Filters
2. Order-Statistics Filters

**Smoothing Linear Filters**

- Linear spatial filter is just the average of the pixels contained in the neighborhood of the filter mask.
- Sometimes it is called "averaging filters".
- The idea is substituting the value of every pixel in an image by the average of the gray levels in the neighborhood defined by the filter mask.
- The general implementation for filtering an MxN image with a weighted averaging filter of size mxn is given by the expression
-

$$g(x,y)=\frac{\sum_{s=-a}^{a}\sum_{t=-b}^{b} w(s,t)f(x+s,y+t)}{\sum_{s=-a}^{a}\sum_{t=-b}^{b} w(s,t)}$$

$$\frac{1}{9}\times\begin{bmatrix}1&1&1\\1&1&1\\1&1&1\end{bmatrix}\qquad\qquad\frac{1}{16}\times\begin{bmatrix}1&2&1\\2&4&2\\1&2&1\end{bmatrix}$$

Standard average Weighted average

Two 3x3 Smoothing Linear Filters

$$\frac{1}{25} \times \frac{1}{?} \times \begin{bmatrix} 1 & 1 & 1 & 1 & 1 \\ 1 & 1 & 1 & 1 & 1 \\ 1 & 1 & 1 & 1 & 1 \\ 1 & 1 & 1 & 1 & 1 \\ 1 & 1 & 1 & 1 & 1 \end{bmatrix}$$

5x5 Smoothing Linear Filters

## Result of Smoothing Linear Filters

**Original Image**

**Using 3*3 mask**

**Using 5*5 mask**

**Using 7*7 mask**

**Order-Statistics Filters**

Order-statistics filters are nonlinear spatial filters whose response is based on ordering or ranking the pixels contained in the image area included by the filter, and then swapping the value of the center pixel with the value determined by the ranking result.

- Best-known as "median filter"

**Process of Median filter**

- Corp region of neighborhood
- Sort the values of the pixel in our region
- In the MxN mask the median is MxN div 2 +1

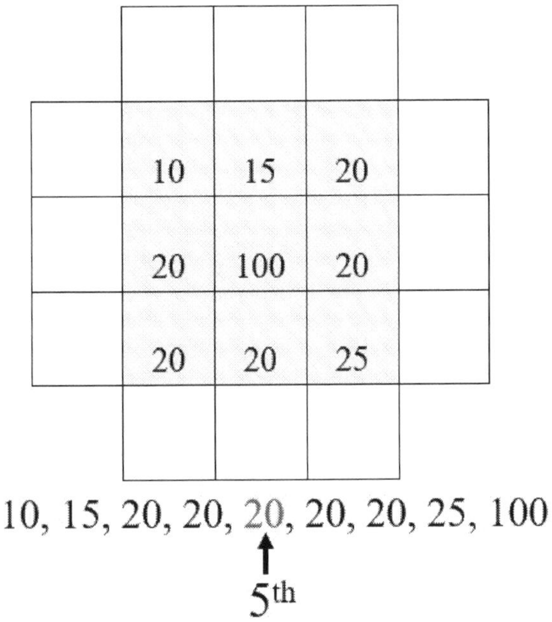

**Result of median filter**

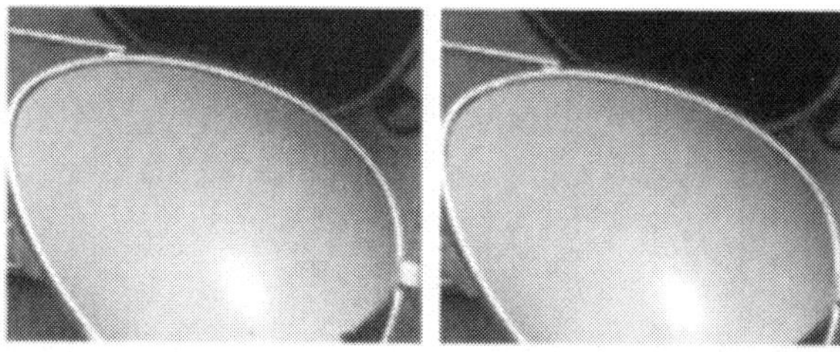

Noise from Glass effect     Remove noise by median filter

***Sharpening Spatial Filters***

- The principal objective of sharpening is to highpoint fine detail in an image or to enhance feature that has been blurred, either in error or as a natural effect of a specific method of image acquisition.
- The image blurring is accomplished in the spatial domain by pixel averaging in a neighborhood.
- Since averaging is similar to integration.
- Sharpening could be accomplished by spatial differentiation.

***Definition for a first derivative***

- *A basic definition of the first-order derivative of a one-dimensional function f(x)* ***is***
- $$\frac{\partial f}{\partial x} = f(x+1) - f(x)$$
- Must be zero in flat segments
- Must be nonzero at the onset of a gray-level step or ramp; and
- Must be nonzero along ramps.

***Definition for a second derivative***

*We define a second-order derivative as the difference*

$$\frac{\partial^2 f}{\partial x^2} = f(x+1) + f(x-1) - 2f(x).$$

- Must be zero in flat areas;
- Must be nonzero at the onset and end of a gray-level step or ramp;
- Must be zero along ramps of constant slope

***Analyze***

$1^{st}$ make thick edge and

$2^{nd}$ make thin edge

- The $1^{st}$-order derivative is nonzero along the whole ramp, while the $2^{nd}$-order derivative is nonzero only at the start and end of the ramp.
- The reply at and around the point is much stronger for the $2^{nd}$- than for the $1^{st}$-order derivative

# MATLAB Source Code For Image Enhancement in Spatial Filtering

```
clc;
clear all;
close all;
a=imread('C:\Users\natheem\Desktop\images\mri.jpg');
b=double(a)+50;
subplot(3,3,1);
imshow(a);
title('original image');
subplot(3,3,2);
imshow(uint8(b));
title('enhanced image');
b1=double(a-70);
subplot(3,3,3);
imshow(uint8(b1));
title('brightness suppressed image');
e=a*.5;
f=a*.20;
```

```
subplot(3,3,4);

imshow(e);

title('increased in contrast');

subplot(3,3,5);

imshow(f);

title('decreased in contrast');

h1=1/9*ones(3,3);

h2=1/25*ones(5,5);

b1=conv2(a,h1,'same');

b2=conv2(a,h2,'same');

subplot(3,3,6);

imshow(uint8(b1));

title('output usins 3*3 mask');

subplot(3,3,7);

imshow(uint8(b2));

title('output using 5*5 mask');
```

# Result

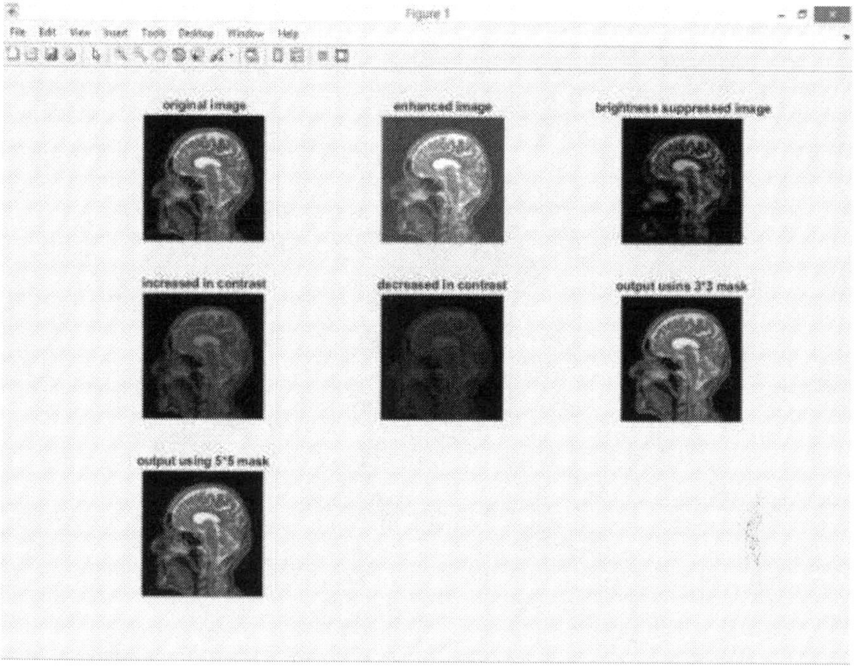

Figure 1
File Edit View Insert Tools Desktop Window Help
original image
enhanced image
brightness suppressed image
increased in contrast
decreased in contrast
output usins 3*3 mask
output using 5*5 mask

**MATLAB Source Code for using separate figure**

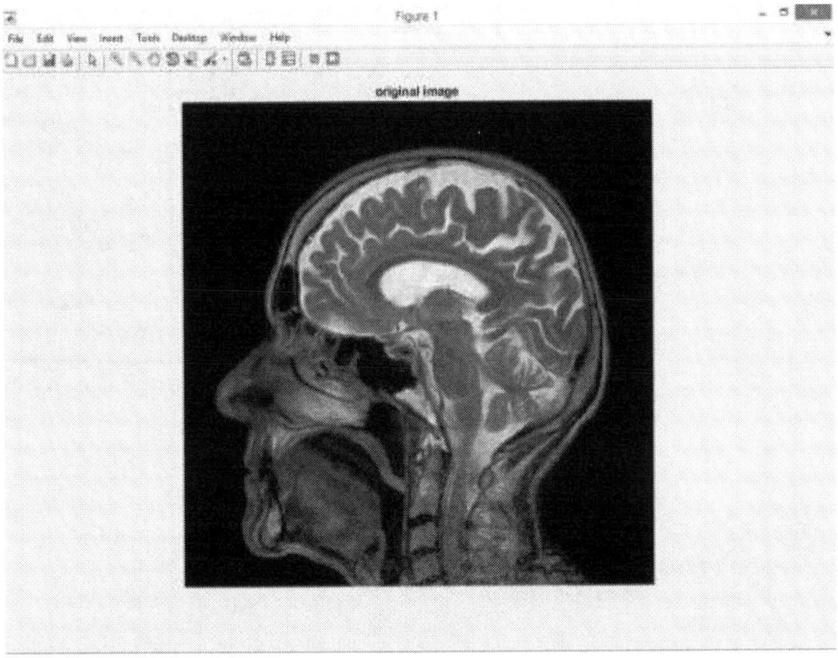


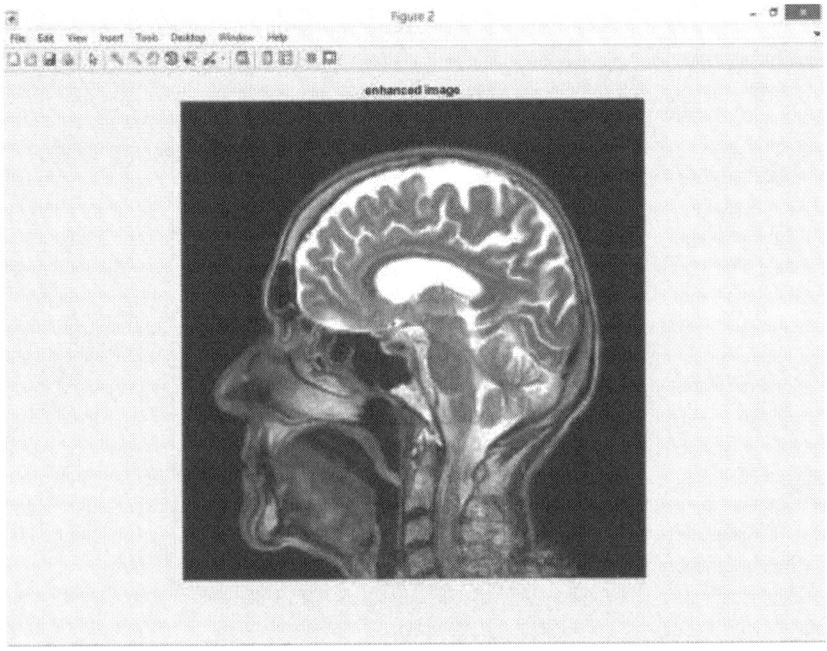

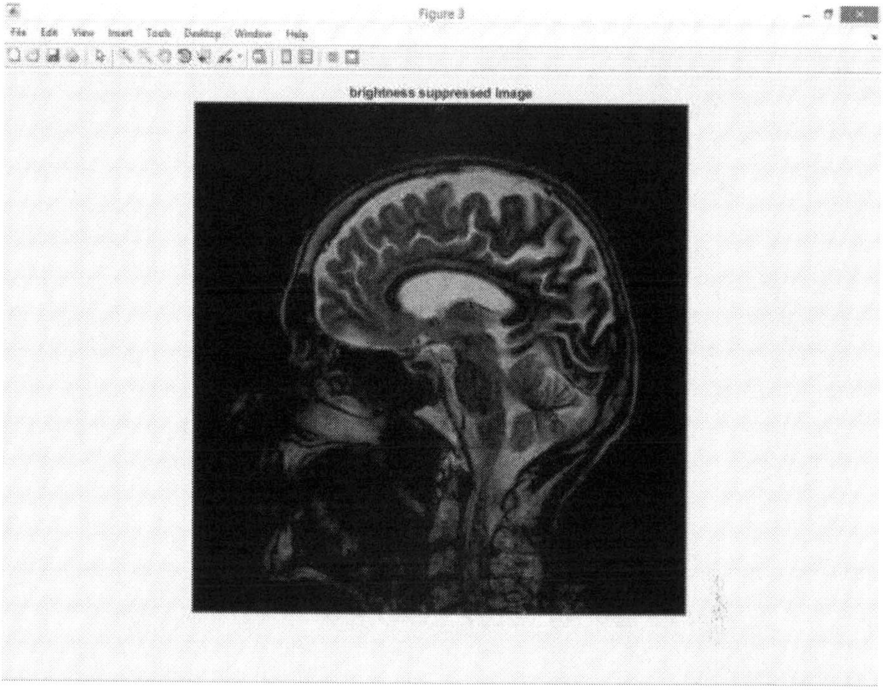
Figure 3
File Edit View Insert Tools Desktop Window Help
brightness suppressed image

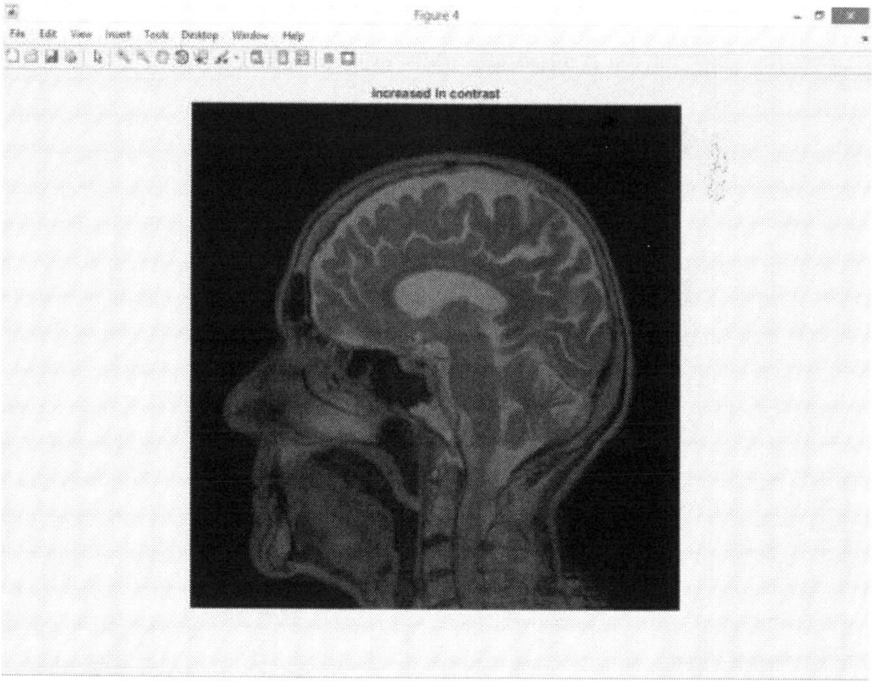
Figure 4
File Edit View Insert Tools Desktop Window Help
increased in contrast

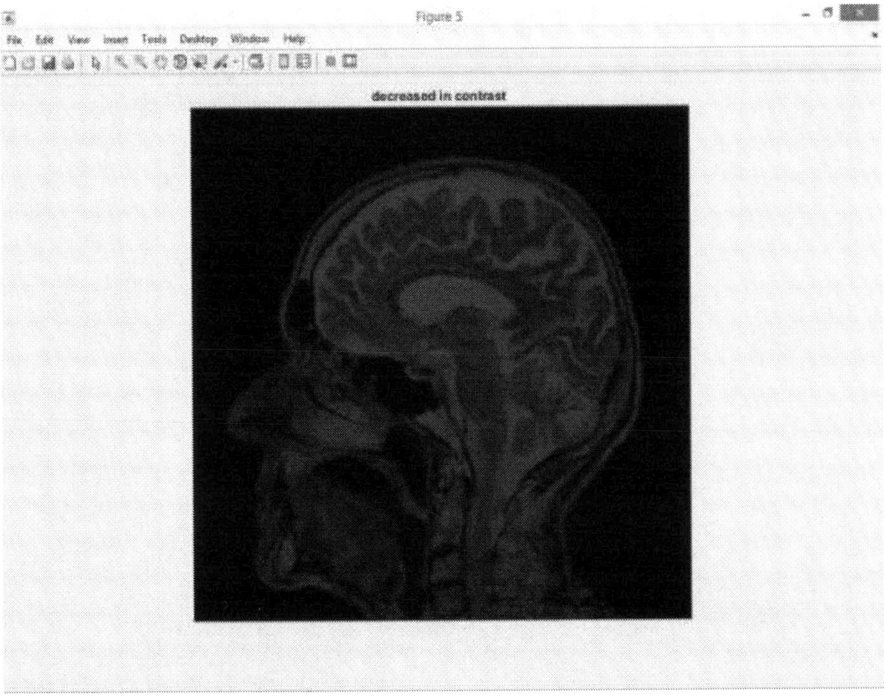
Figure 5
File Edit View Insert Tools Desktop Window Help
decreased in contrast

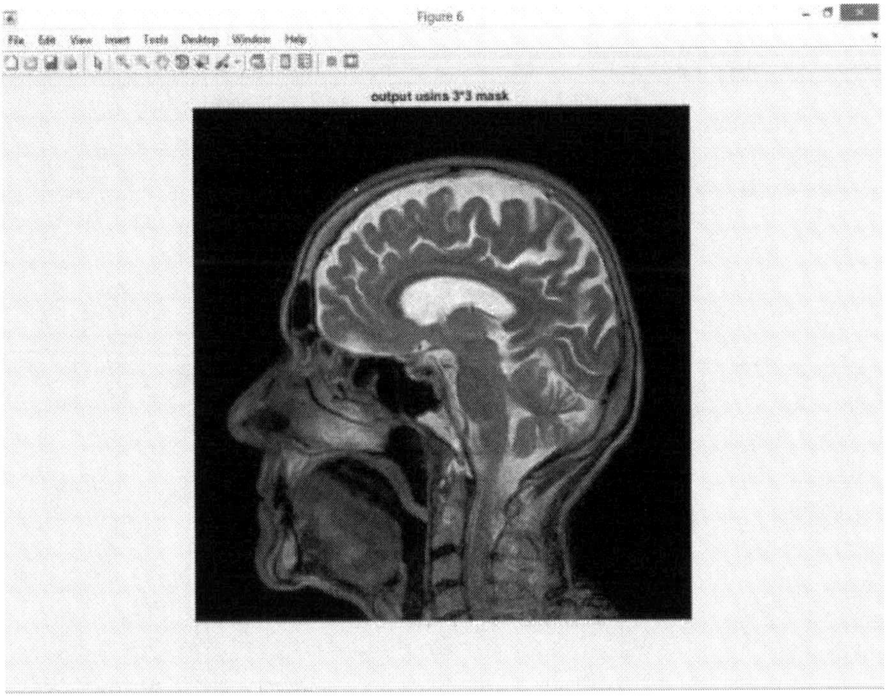
Figure 6
File Edit View Insert Tools Desktop Window Help
output usins 3*3 mask

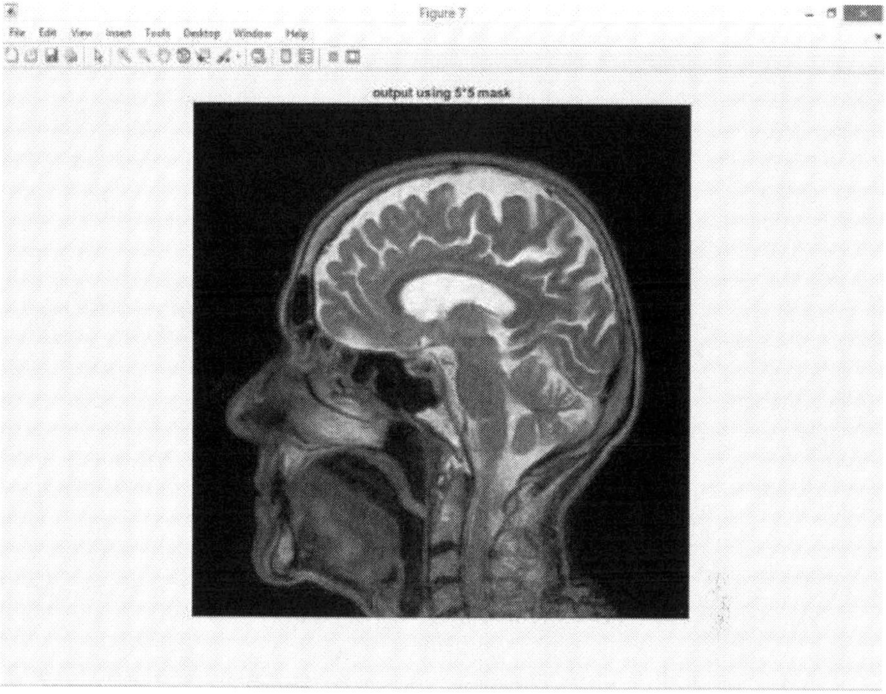
Figure 7
File Edit View Insert Tools Desktop Window Help
output using 5*5 mask

# CHAPTER 7.

## ENHANCEMENT IN FREQUENCY FILTER

**Enhancement in Frequency Domain Filtering**

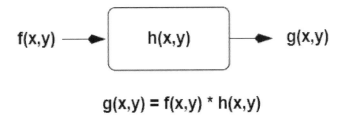

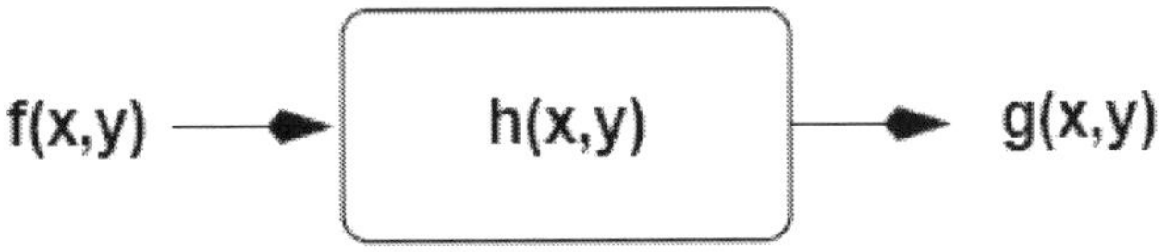


$$g(x,y) = f(x,y) * h(x,y)$$

Spatial Domain

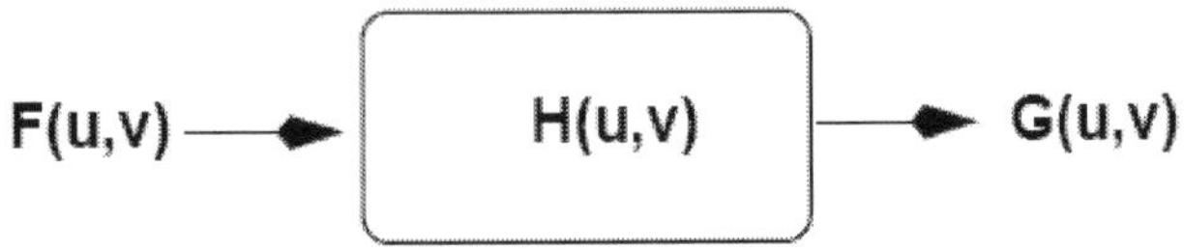


$$G(u,v) = F(u,v)\, H(u,v)$$

$$(\, g(x,y) = F^{-1}(F(u,v)\, H(u,v))\, )$$

Frequency Domain

**Major filter categories**

Naturally, filters are categorized by examining their properties in the frequency domain:

1) Low-pass
2) High-pass
3) Band-pass
4) Band-stop

**Example**

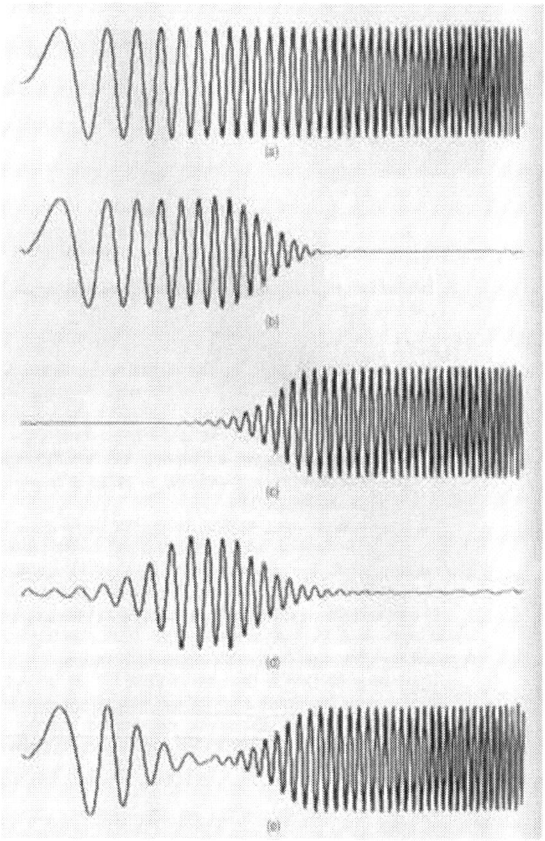

**Original** signal

**Low-pass** filtered

**High-pass** filtered

**Band-pass** filtered

**Band-stop** filtered

**Low-pass filters** (Smoothing Filters):

- Low-pass filters also known as called Smoothing Filters
- Preserve low frequencies - useful for **noise suppression**

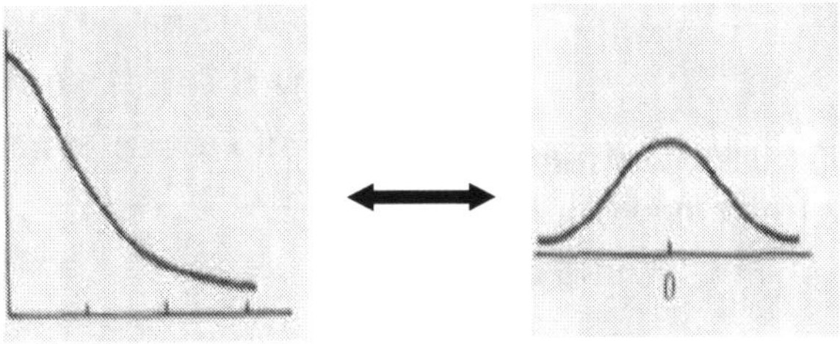


**Example:**

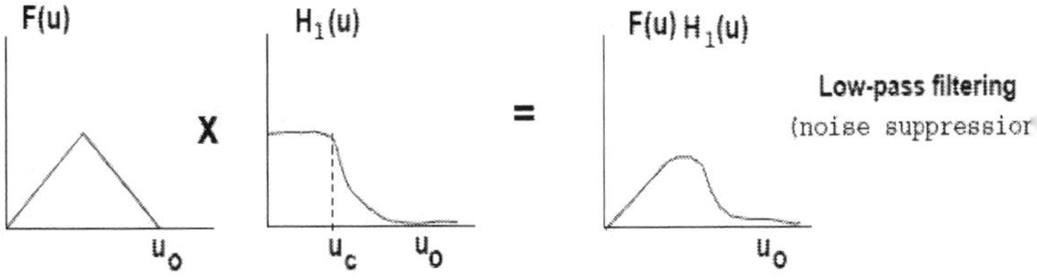


**High-pass filters** (Sharpening Filters)

- High-pass filters also known as called Sharpening Filters
- Preserves high frequencies - useful for edge detection

Example

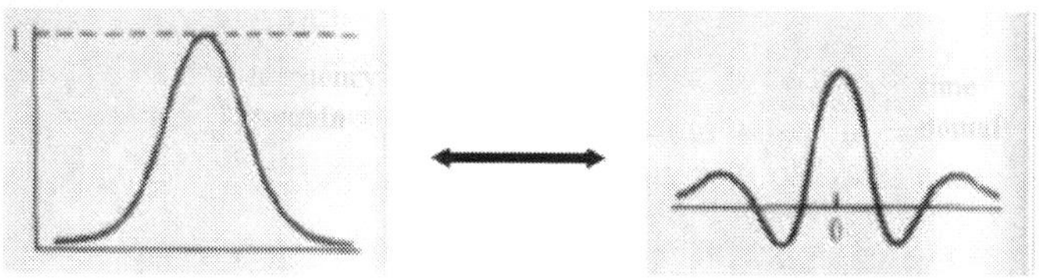

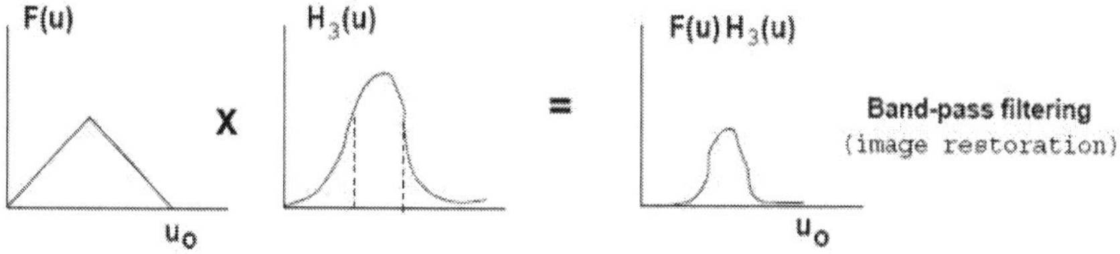


**Band-Stop filters**

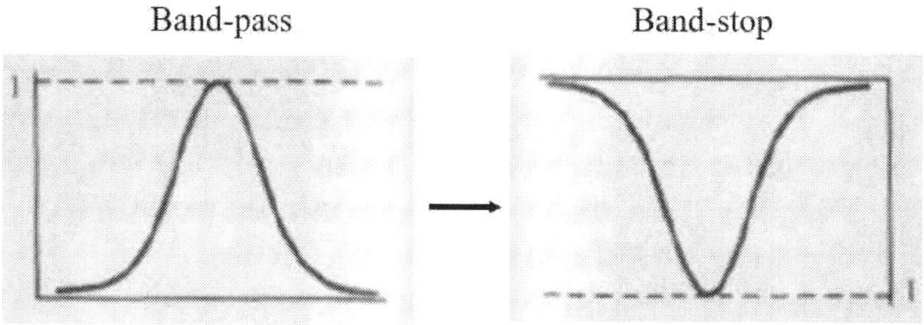

## Frequency Domain Methods

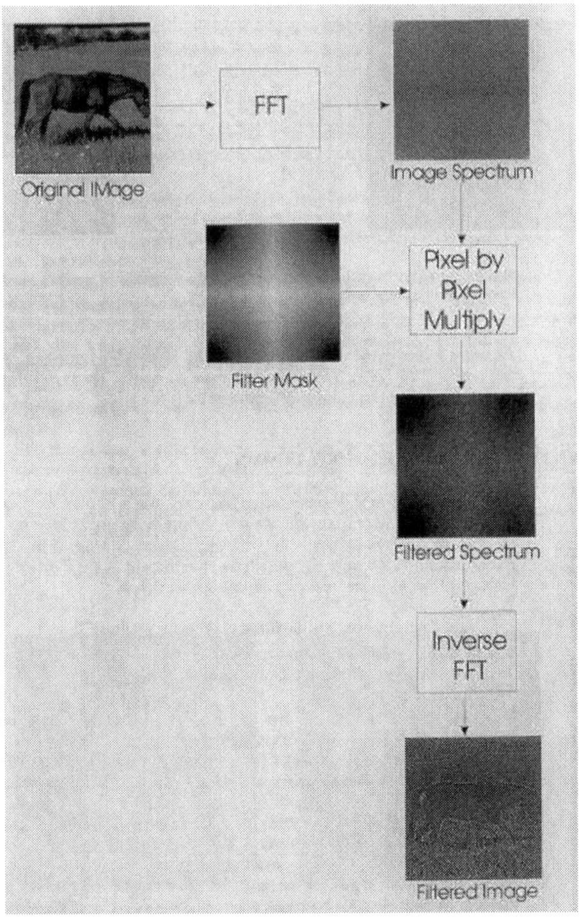


$$f(x,y) * h(x,y) = g(x,y)$$

$$F(u,v)\ H(u,v) = G(u,v)$$

**Case 1:** h(u,v) is stated in the frequency domain.

**Case 2:** h(x,y) is stated in the spatial domain.

**Frequency domain filtering:**

**STEPS**

$$f(x, y) * h(x, y) = g(x, y)$$

1. Given an input image $f(x, y)$ of size $M \times N$, obtain the padding parameters $P$ and $Q$ from Eqs. (4.6-31) and (4.6-32). Typically, we select $P = 2M$ and $Q = 2N$.
2. Form a padded image, $f_p(x, y)$, of size $P \times Q$ by appending the necessary number of zeros to $f(x, y)$.
3. Multiply $f_p(x, y)$ by $(-1)^{x+y}$ to center its transform.
4. Compute the DFT, $F(u, v)$, of the image from step 3.

$$F(u,v) = R(u,v) + jI(u,v)$$

5. Generate a real, symmetric filter function, $H(u, v)$, of size $P \times Q$ with center at coordinates $(P/2, Q/2)$.† Form the product $G(u, v) = H(u, v)F(u, v)$

$$G(u,v) = F(u,v)H(u,v) = H(u,v)\,R(u,v) + jH(u,v)I(u,v)$$

6. Obtain the processed image:

$$g_p(x, y) = \left\{\text{real}\left[\Im^{-1}[G(u, v)]\right]\right\}(-1)^{x+y}$$

where the real part is selected in order to ignore parasitic complex components resulting from computational inaccuracies, and the subscript $p$ indicates that we are dealing with padded arrays.

7. Obtain the final processed result, $g(x, y)$, by extracting the $M \times N$ region from the top, left quadrant of $g_p(x, y)$.

**Types of Low Pass (LP) Filters**

1. Ideal low-pass filter (ILPF)
2. Butterworth low-pass filter (BLPF)
3. Gaussian low-pass filter (GLPF)

**Types of High Pass (LP) Filters**

1. Ideal high-pass filter (IHPF)
2. Butterworth high-pass filter (BHPF)
3. Gaussian high-pass filter (GHPF)
4. Difference of Gaussians
5. Unsharp Masking and High Boost filtering

```
%LOW PASS FILTER

clc;

clear all;

close all;

a=imread('coins.png');

[m,n]=size(a);

mask=zeros(m,n);

for i=150:180

   for j=210:240

      mask (i,j)=i;

   end

end

c=fftshift(mask);

b=fft2(a);

d=b.*c;

e=abs(ifft2(b));

figure(1);

subplot(3,3,1);
```

```
imshow(a);

title('original image');

subplot(3,3,2);

imshow(uint8(e));

title('low passs filtered image');

subplot(3,3,3);

imshow(mask);

subplot(3,3,4);

imshow(c);

title('mask after fftshift ooperation');

%HIGH PASS FILTER

a=imread('coins.png');

[m,n]=size(a);

mask=ones(m,n);

for i=150:180

   for j=210:240

      mask (i,j)=0;

   end

end

c=fftshift(mask);
```

```
b=fft2(a);
d=b.*c;
e=abs(ifft2(b));
subplot(3,3,5);
imshow(a);
title('original image');
subplot(3,3,6);
imshow(uint8(e));
title('high pass filtered image');
subplot(3,3,7);
imshow(mask);
subplot(3,3,8);
imshow(c);
title('high pass filter mask');
%BAND PASS  PASS FILTER
a=imread('coins.png');
[m,n]=size(a);
mask=zeros(m,n);
for i=160:170
   for j=260:230
```

```
    mask (i,j)=0;
  end
end
c=fftshift(mask);
b=fft2(a);
d=b.*c;
e=abs(ifft2(b));
figure(2);
subplot(2,2,1);
imshow(a);
title('original image');
subplot(2,2,2);
imshow(uint8(e));
title('band   pass filtered image');
subplot(2,2,3);
imshow(uint8(mask));
subplot(2,2,4);
imshow(uint8(c));
title('mask after fftshift ooperation');
% BAND REJECT FILTER
```

```
a=imread('coins.png');
[m,n]=size(a);
mask=ones(m,n);
for i=150:180
   for j=210:240
      mask(i,j)=0;
   end
end
c=fftshift(mask);
b=fft2(a);
d=b.*c;
e=abs(ifft2(b));
figure(3);
subplot(2,2,1);
imshow(a);
title('original image');
subplot(2,2,2);
imshow(uint8 (e));
title('band reject pass filtered image');
subplot(2,2,3);
```

```
imshow(mask);

subplot(2,2,4);

imshow(c);

title('high pass filter mask');
```

**Result**

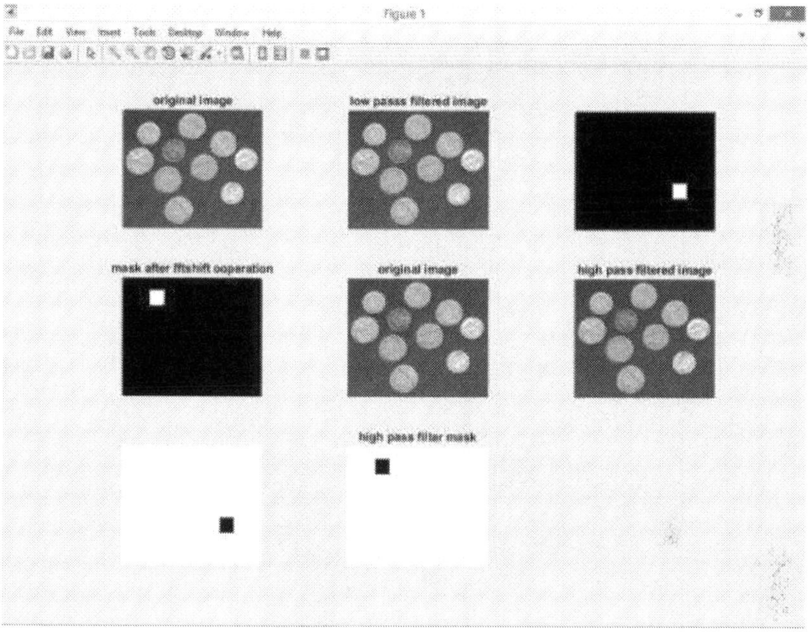

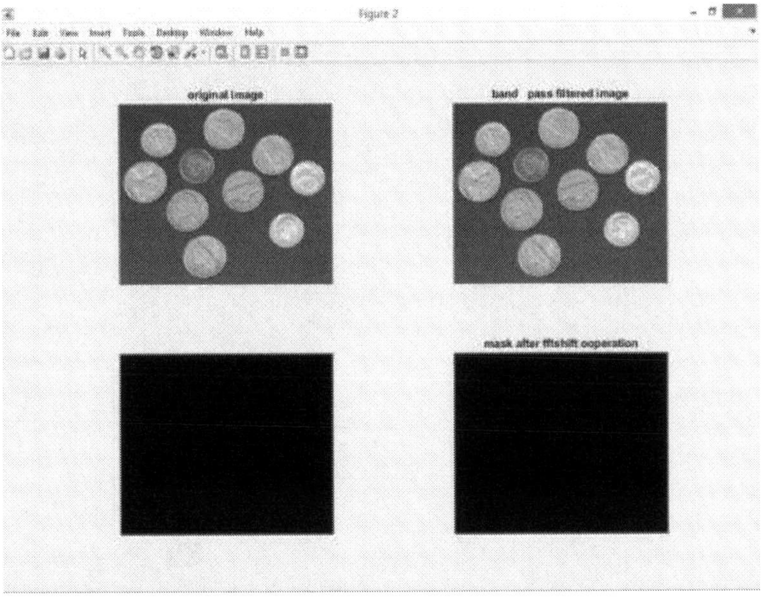
Figure 2
File Edit View Insert Tools Desktop Window Help
original image
band pass filtered image
mask after fftshift ooperation

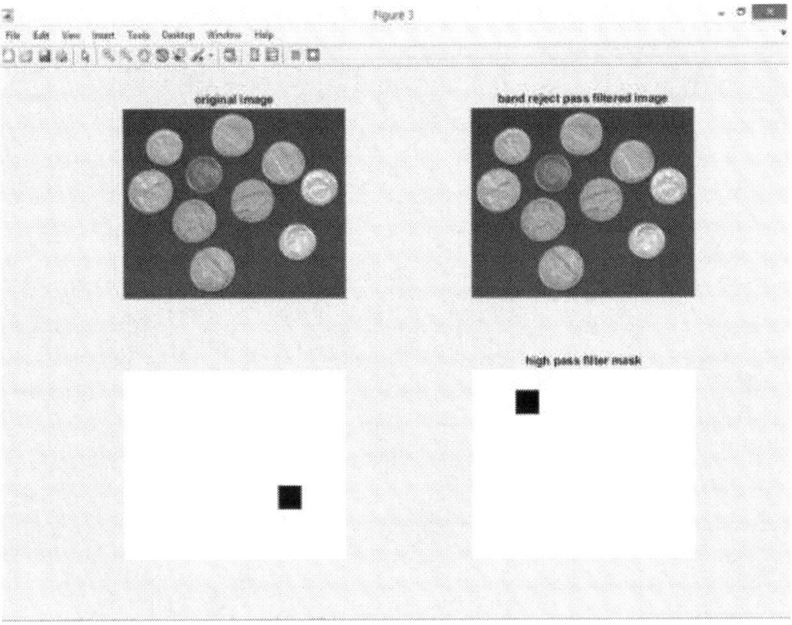
Figure 3
File Edit View Insert Tools Desktop Window Help
original image
band reject pass filtered image
high pass filter mask

# CHAPTER 8.

## COLOR IMAGE PROCESSING

**Why use color in image processing?**

Color is a powerful descriptor.

- Object identification and extraction
- **Example:** Face detection using skin colors

- Humans can discern thousands of color shades and intensities
- Human discern only two dozen shades of grays

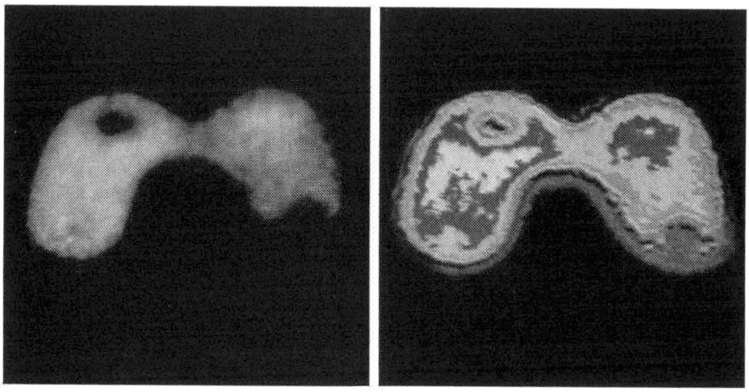

**Types of color image processing**

1. Pseudo-color processing
2. Full color processing

**Full color processing**

Images are acquired from full-color sensor or equipment

**Pseudo-color processing**

- In the past period, color sensors and processing hardware are not available
- Colors are assigned to a range of monochrome intensities
- 

**Color fundamentals**

1) Color models
2) Pseudo-color image processing
3) Color transformations
4) Smoothing and sharpening

## 1) COLOR FUNDAMENTALS

**Physical phenomenon**

Physical nature of color is identified

**Psysio-psychological phenomenon**

How human brain see and understand color?

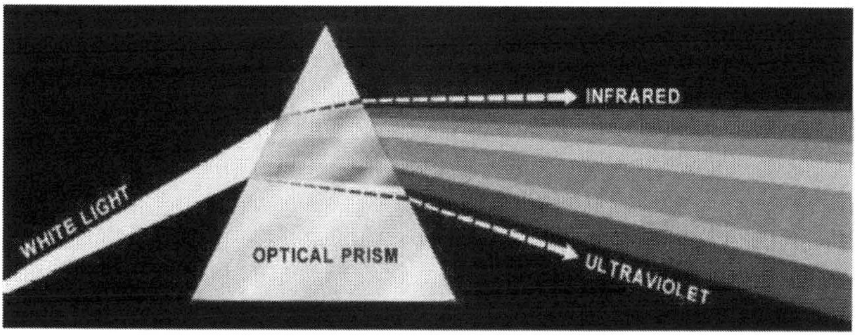


FIGURE 6.1 Color spectrum seen by passing white light through a prism. (Courtesy of the General Electric Co., Lamp Business Division.)

## Visible light

Chromatic light distance the electromagnetic spectrum (EM) from 400 to 700 nm

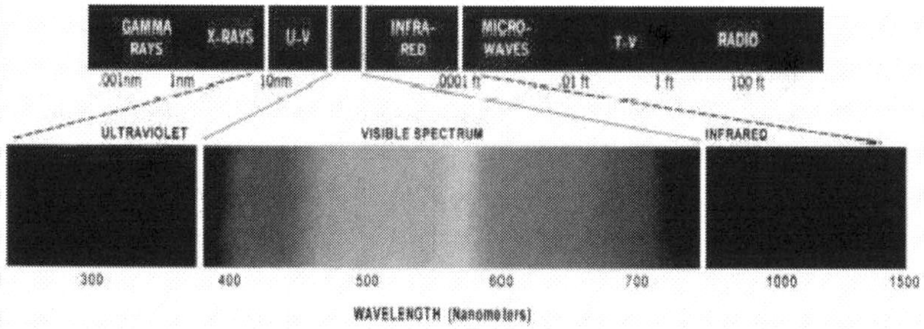


FIGURE 6.2 Wavelengths comprising the visible range of the electromagnetic spectrum. (Courtesy of the General Electric Co., Lamp Business Division.)

The color that human perceive in an object = the light reflected from the object

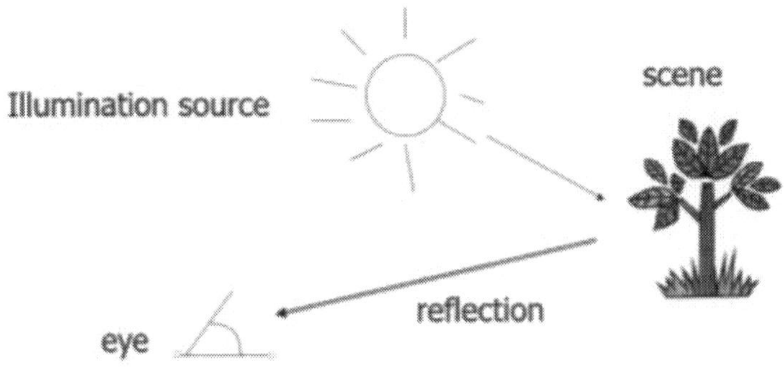


**Radiance**:

Total amount of energy that flow from the light source, measured in watts (W)

**Luminance:**

Amount of energy an observer *perceives* from a light source, measured in lumens far infrared light: high radiance, but 0 luminance

**Brightness:**

Subjective descriptor that is hard to measure, alike to the achromatic view of intensity

- **6~7M** Cones are the sensors in the eye
- 3 principal sensing categories in eyes
- Red light 65%, green light 33%, and blue light 2%

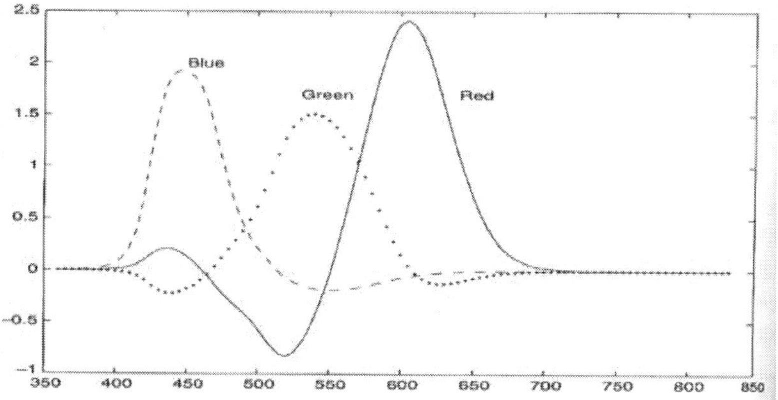

**FIGURE 13.1** *RGB color-matching functions (CIE, 1931).*

In 1931, CIE (International Commission on Illumination) defines specific wavelength values to the

**Primary colors**

- B = 435.8 nm, G = 546.1 nm, R = 700 nm
- However, we know that <u>no single color</u> may be called red, green, or blue

**Secondary colors**:

- ✓ G+B=Cyan,
- ✓ R+G=Yellow,
- ✓ R+B=Magenta

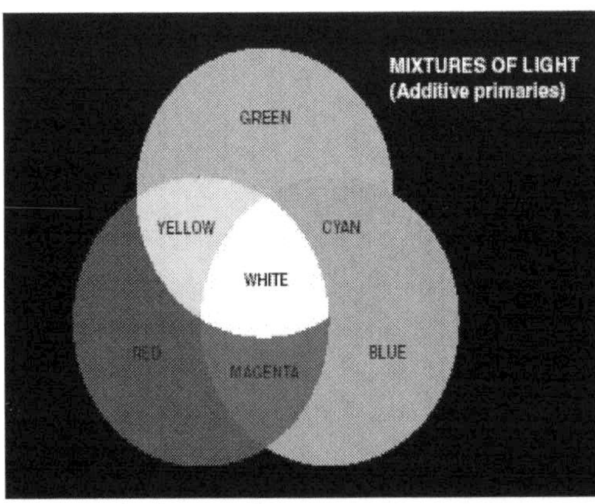


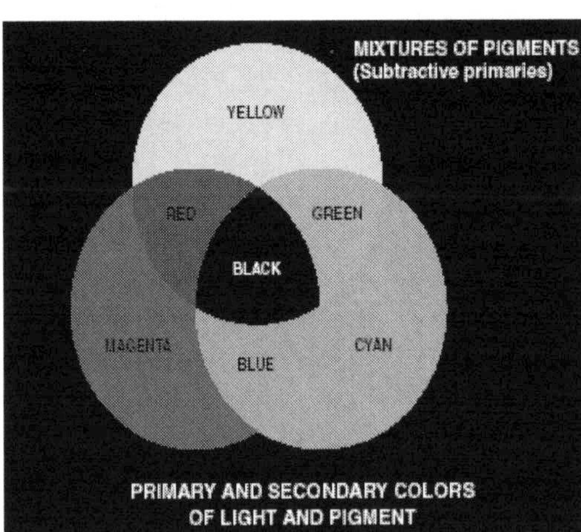


PRIMARY AND SECONDARY COLORS
OF LIGHT AND PIGMENT

**Color TV**

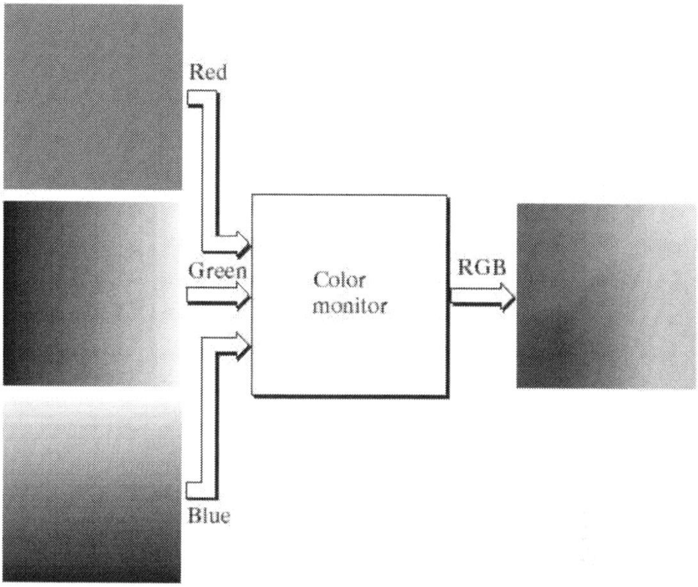


## 2) COLOR MODELS

Color model, color space, color system

a. Specify colors in a standard way

b. A coordinate system that each color is represented by a single point

- RGB model
- CYM model
- CYMK model

  } Suitable for hardware or applications

- HSI model

  - match the human description

**RGB color model**

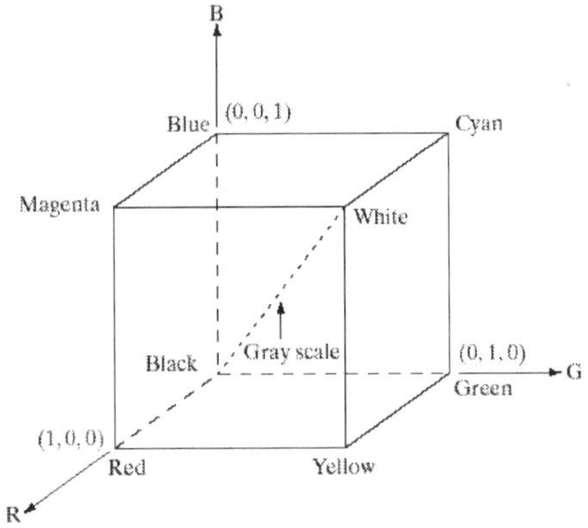


**Pixel depth:**

The number of bits used to represent each pixel in RGB space

**Full-color image:**

24-bit RGB color image

(R, G, B) = (8 bits, 8 bits, 8 bits)

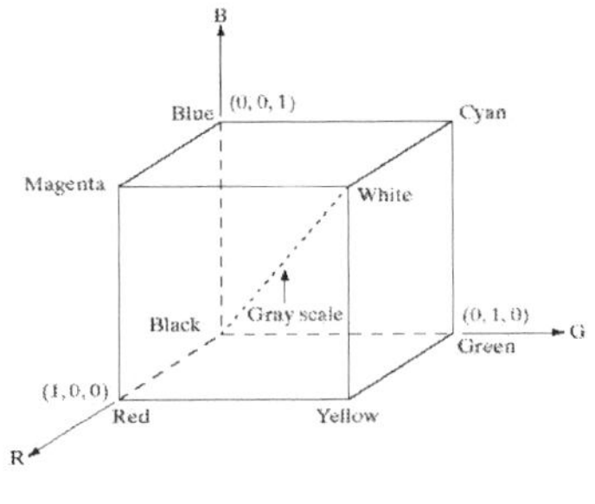


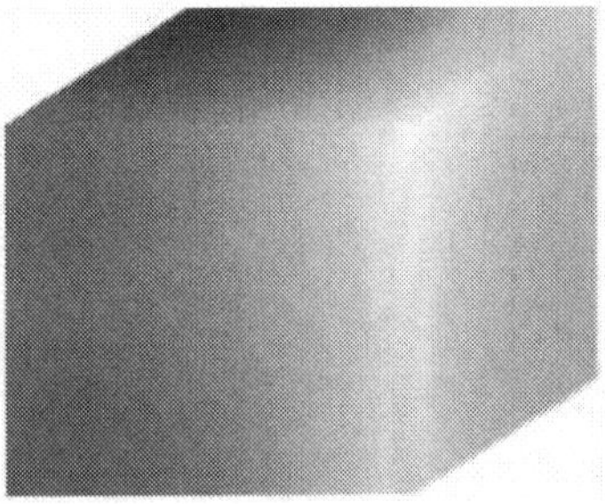

**CMY model (+Black = CMYK)**

- ✓ **CMY:** secondary colors of light, or primary colors of pigments
- ✓ Used to produce hardcopy output

$$\begin{bmatrix} C \\ M \\ Y \end{bmatrix} = \begin{bmatrix} 1 \\ 1 \\ 1 \end{bmatrix} - \begin{bmatrix} R \\ G \\ B \end{bmatrix}$$

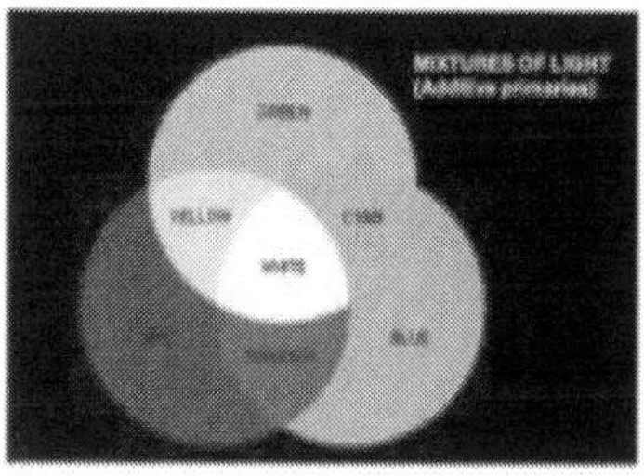

**HSI color model**

- ✓ Will you describe a color using its R, G, B components?
- ✓ Human describe a color by its hue, saturation, and brightness

1. **Hue :** color attribute
2. **Saturation:** purity of color (white->0, primary color->1)
3. **Brightness:** achromatic notion of intensity

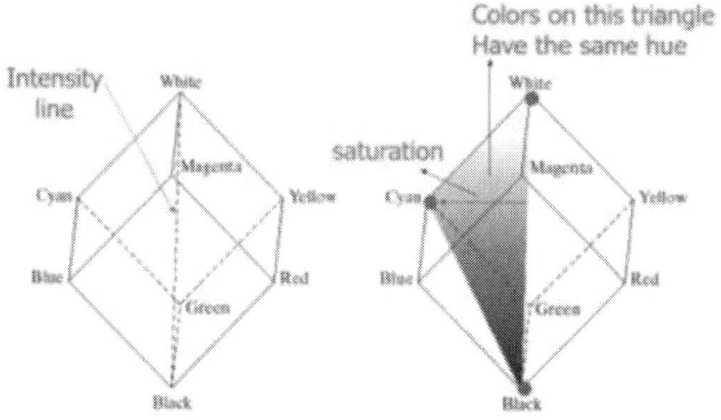


Fig. RGB -> HSI model

**Pseudo-color image processing**

- Assign colors to gray values based on a specified criterion
- For human visualization and understanding of gray-scale events
- Intensity slicing
- Gray level to color conversions

**Application 1**

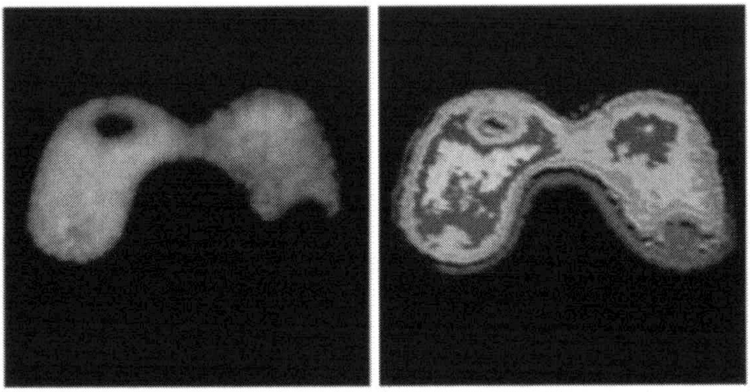

Radiation test pattern → 8 color regions

**Application 2**

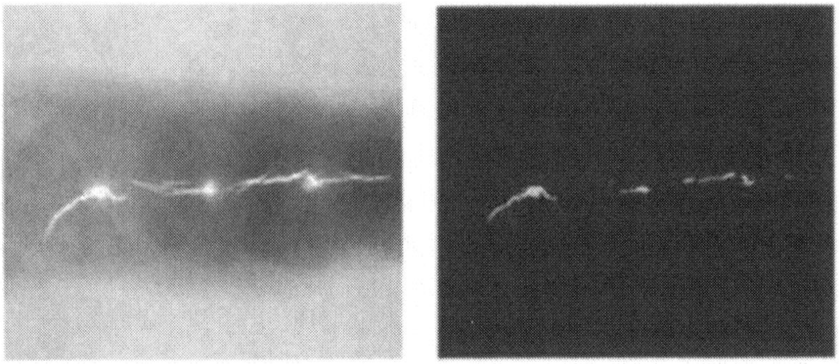

X-ray image of a weld

# Application 3

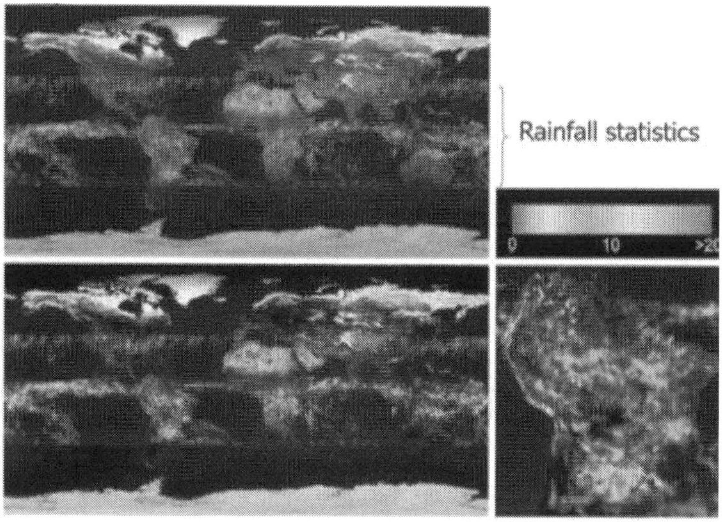

## Gray level to color transformation

Intensity slicing: piecewise linear transformation

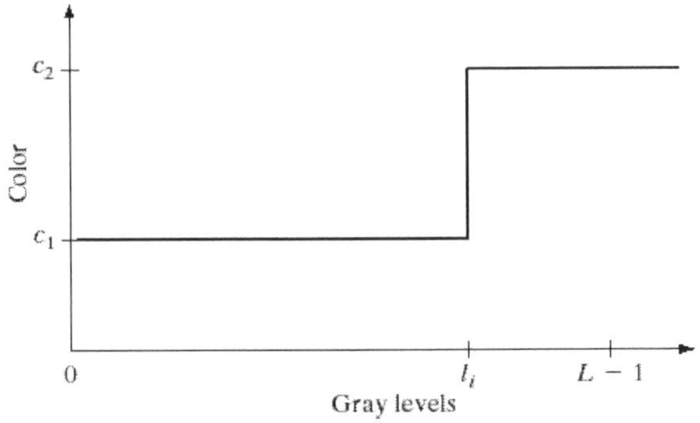


General Gray level to color transformation

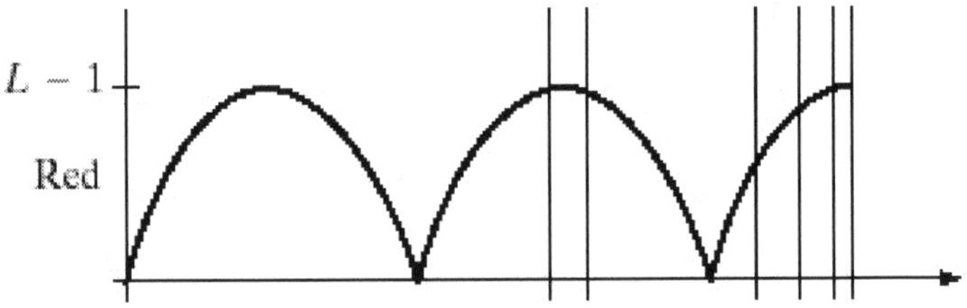


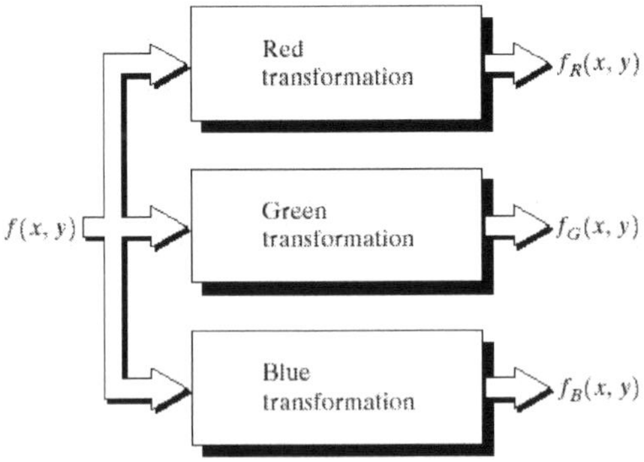


**FIGURE 6.23** Functional block diagram for pseudocolor image processing. $f_R$, $f_G$, and $f_B$ are fed into the corresponding red, green, and blue inputs of an RGB color monitor.

### 3) Color transformation

- Similar to gray scale transformation

  g(x,y)=T[f(x,y)]

- Color transformation

$$s_i = T_i(r_1, r_2, \ldots, r_n), \quad i = 1,2,\ldots,n$$

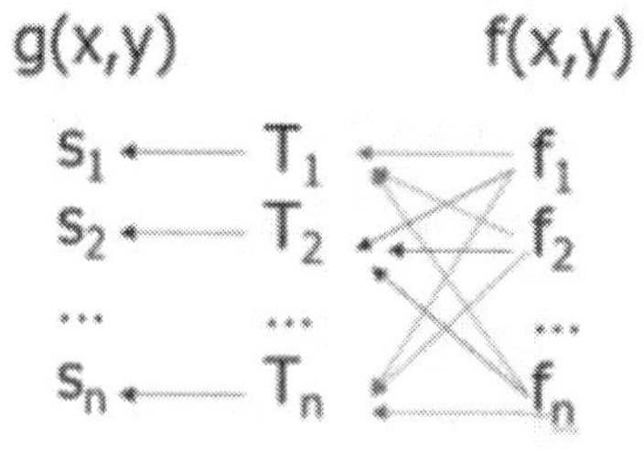


RGB ⇔CMY (K) ⇔ HSI

- ➢ **Theoretically,** any transformation can be performed in any color model
- ➢ **Practically,** some operations are better suitable to specific color model

**Example:**

$g(x,y)=k\ f(x,y), \quad 0<k<1$

1) HSI color space

- Intensity: $s_3 = k\ r_3$
- Note: transform to HSI requires complex operations

2) RGB color space

- For each R,G,B component: $s_i = k\ r_i$

3) CMY color space

- For each C,M,Y component:
- $s_i = k\, r_i + (1-k)$

## Color image smoothing

Neighborhood processing

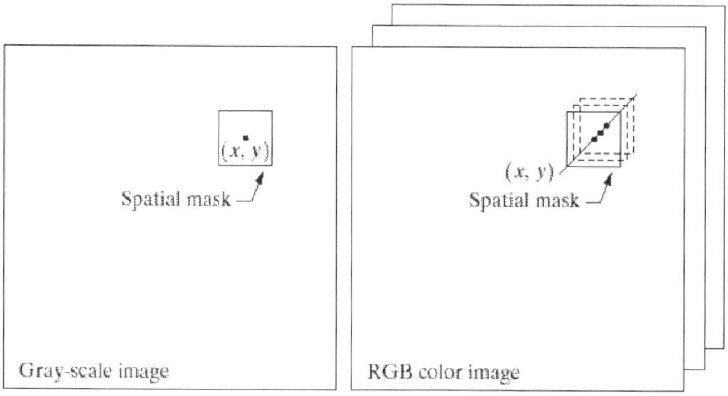


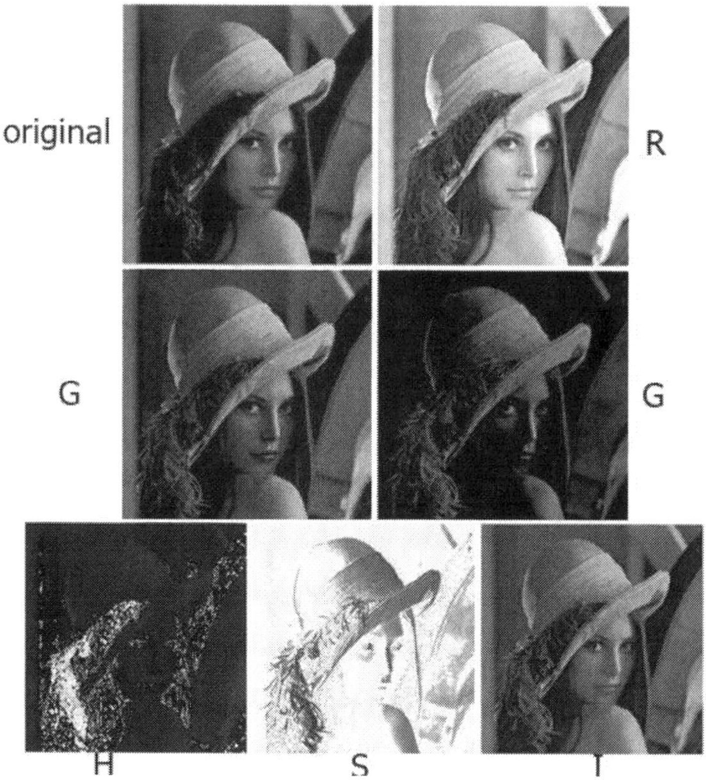

```
clc;

clear all;

close all;

a=imread('peppers.png');

subplot(3,3,1);

imshow(a);

title('original image');

g=rgb2gray(a);

subplot(3,3,2);

imshow(g);

title('gray conversion');

ntsc_img=rgb2ntsc(a);

subplot(3,3,3);

imshow(ntsc_img);

title('ntsc colour space conversion');

ycbcr_img=rgb2ycbcr(a);

subplot(3,3,4);

imshow(ycbcr_img);
```

```
title('ycbcr colour space  conversion');

hsv_img=rgb2hsv(a);

subplot(3,3,5);

imshow(hsv_img);

title('hsv  colour space conversion');

cmy_img=imcomplement(a);

subplot(3,3,6);

imshow(cmy_img);

title('cmy colour  space conversion');

rgb=im2double(a);

r=rgb(:,:,1);

g=rgb(:,:,2);

b=rgb(:,:,3);

num=.5*((r-g)+(r-b));

den=sqrt(r-g).^2+(r-g).*(g-b);

theta=acos(num./(den +eps));

H=theta;

H(b>g)=2*pi-H(b>g);

H=H/(2*pi);

num=min(min(r,g),b);
```

```
den=r+g+b;
den(den==0)=eps;
S=1-3.*num./den;
H(S==0)=0;
I=(r+g+b)/3;
hsi=cat(3,H,S,I);
subplot(3,3,7);
imshow(hsi);
title('HSI');


figure(2);
subplot(2,3,1);
imshow(r);
title('red component');
subplot(2,3,2);
imshow(g);
title('green component');
subplot(2,3,3);
imshow(b);
title('blue component');
```

```
subplot(2,3,4);

imshow(H);

title('hue component');

subplot(2,3,5);

imshow(S);

title('saturation component');

subplot(2,3,6);

imshow(I);

title('brightness component');
```

**OUTPUT**

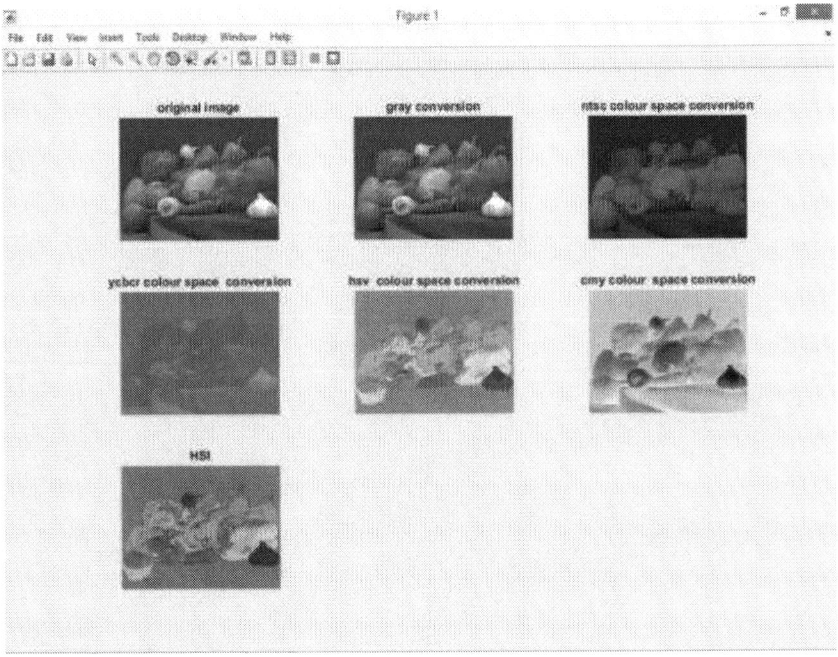
Figure 1
File Edit View Insert Tools Desktop Window Help
original image
gray conversion
ntsc colour space conversion
ycbcr colour space conversion
hsv colour space conversion
cmy colour space conversion
HSI

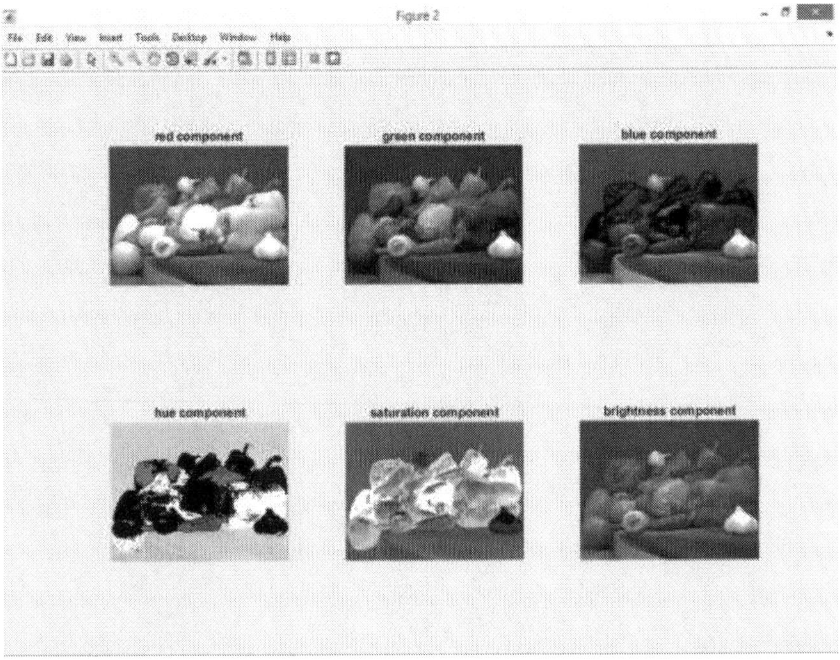
Figure 2
File Edit View Insert Tools Desktop Window Help
red component
green component
blue component
hue component
saturation component
brightness component

## MATLAB PROGRAM USING INDIVIDUAL FIGURE

```
clc;

clear all;

close all;

a=imread('peppers.png');

figure(1);

imshow(a);

title('original image');

g=rgb2gray(a);

figure(2);

imshow(g);

title('gray conversion');

ntsc_img=rgb2ntsc(a);

figure(3);

imshow(ntsc_img);

title('ntsc colour space conversion');

ycbcr_img=rgb2ycbcr(a);

figure(4);

imshow(ycbcr_img);
```

```
title('ycbcr colour space  conversion');

hsv_img=rgb2hsv(a);

figure(5);

imshow(hsv_img);

title('hsv  colour space conversion');

cmy_img=imcomplement(a);

figure(6);

imshow(cmy_img);

title('cmy colour  space conversion');

rgb=im2double(a);

r=rgb(:,:,1);

g=rgb(:,:,2);

b=rgb(:,:,3);

num=.5*((r-g)+(r-b));

den=sqrt(r-g).^2+(r-g).*(g-b);

theta=acos(num./(den +eps));

H=theta;

H(b>g)=2*pi-H(b>g);

H=H/(2*pi);

num=min(min(r,g),b);
```

```
den=r+g+b;

den(den==0)=eps;

S=1-3.*num./den;

H(S==0)=0;

I=(r+g+b)/3;

hsi=cat(3,H,S,I);

figure(7);

imshow(hsi);

title('HSI');


figure(8);

subplot(2,3,1);

imshow(r);

title('red component');

figure(9);

imshow(g);

title('green component');

figure(10);

imshow(b);

title('blue component');
```

```
figure(11);
imshow(H);
title('hue component');
figure(12);
imshow(S);
title('saturation component');
figure(13);
imshow(I);
title('brightness component');
```

# OUTPUT

Figure 1
File Edit View Insert Tools Desktop Window Help
original image

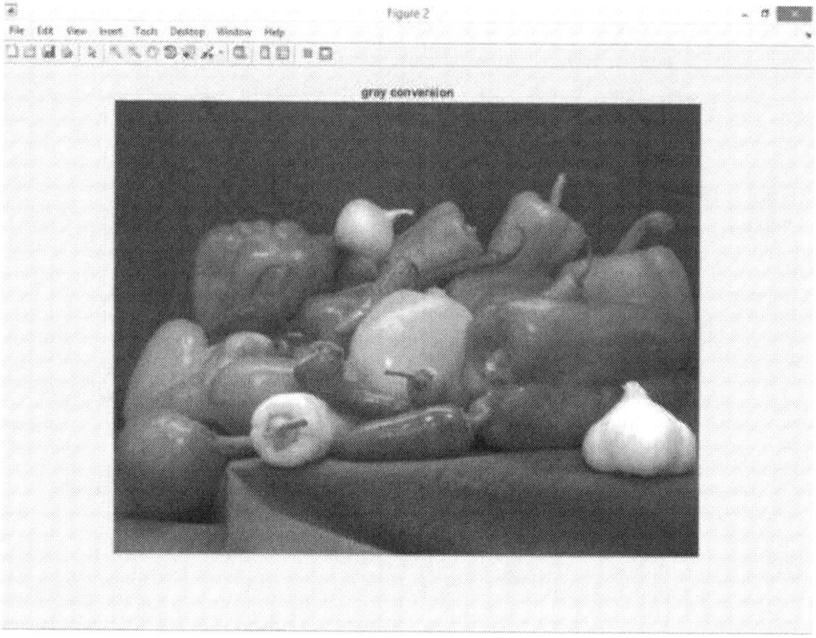
Figure 2
File Edit View Insert Tools Desktop Window Help
gray conversion

Figure 3
File Edit View Insert Tools Desktop Window Help
ntsc colour space conversion

Figure 4
File Edit View Insert Tools Desktop Window Help
ycbcr colour space conversion

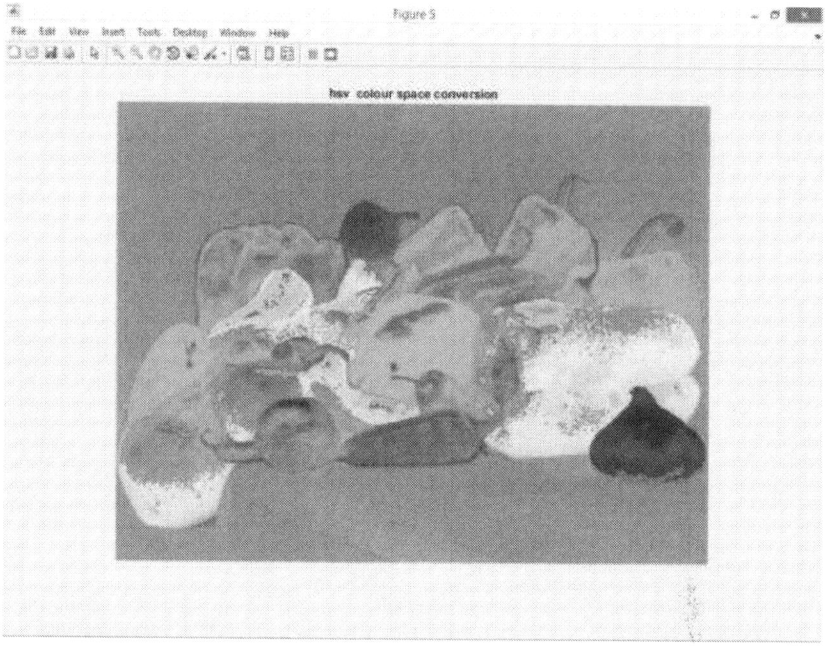
Figure 5
File Edit View Insert Tools Desktop Window Help
hsv colour space conversion

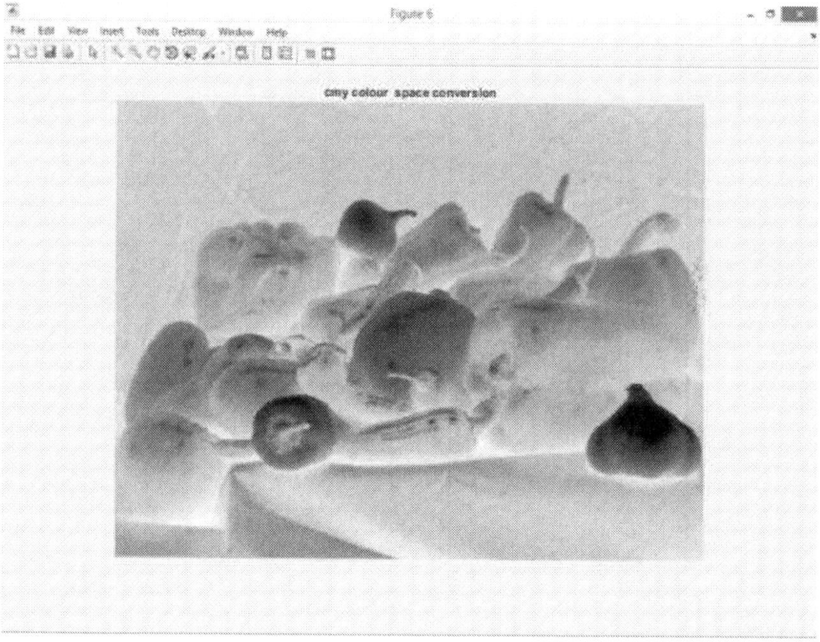
Figure 6
File Edit View Insert Tools Desktop Window Help
cmy colour space conversion

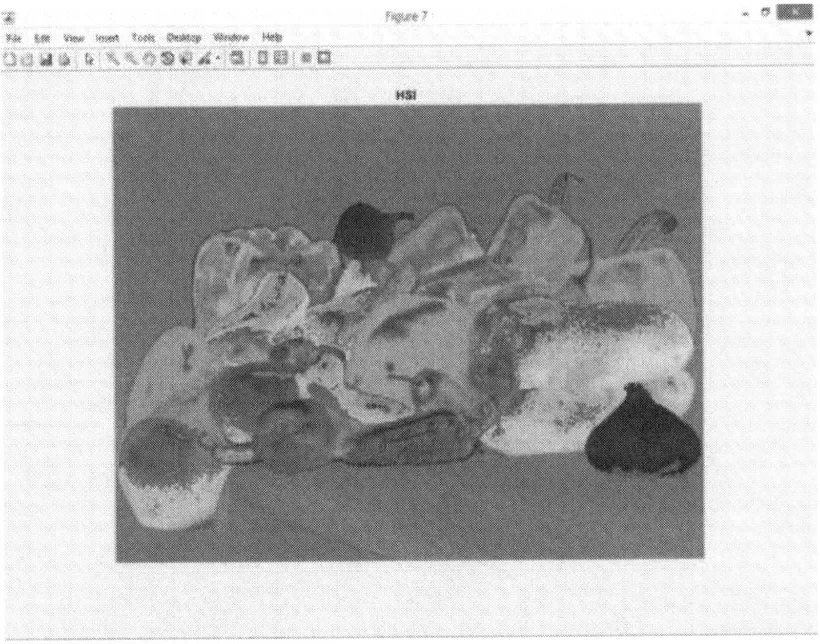
Figure 7
File Edit View Insert Tools Desktop Window Help
HSI

Figure 8
File Edit View Insert Tools Desktop Window Help
red component

Figure 9
File Edit View Insert Tools Desktop Window Help
green component

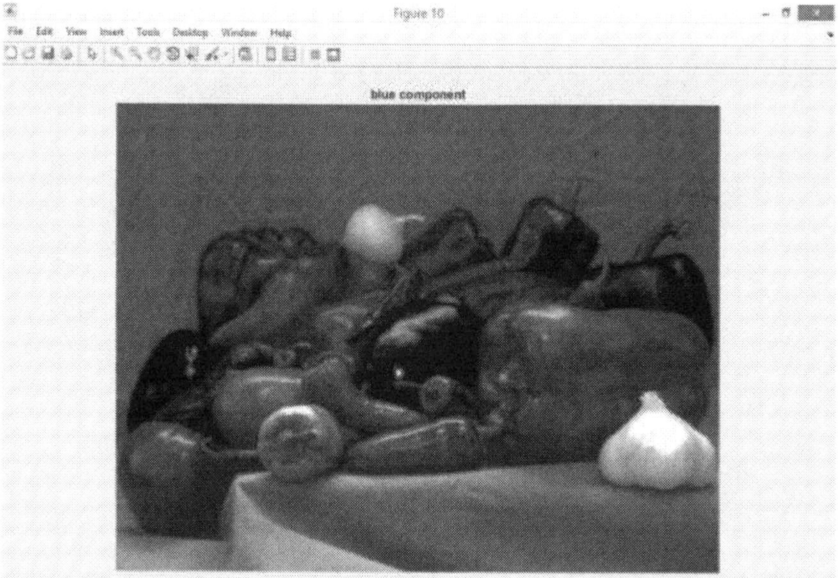
Figure 10
File Edit View Insert Tools Desktop Window Help
blue component

Figure 11
File Edit View Insert Tools Desktop Window Help
hue component

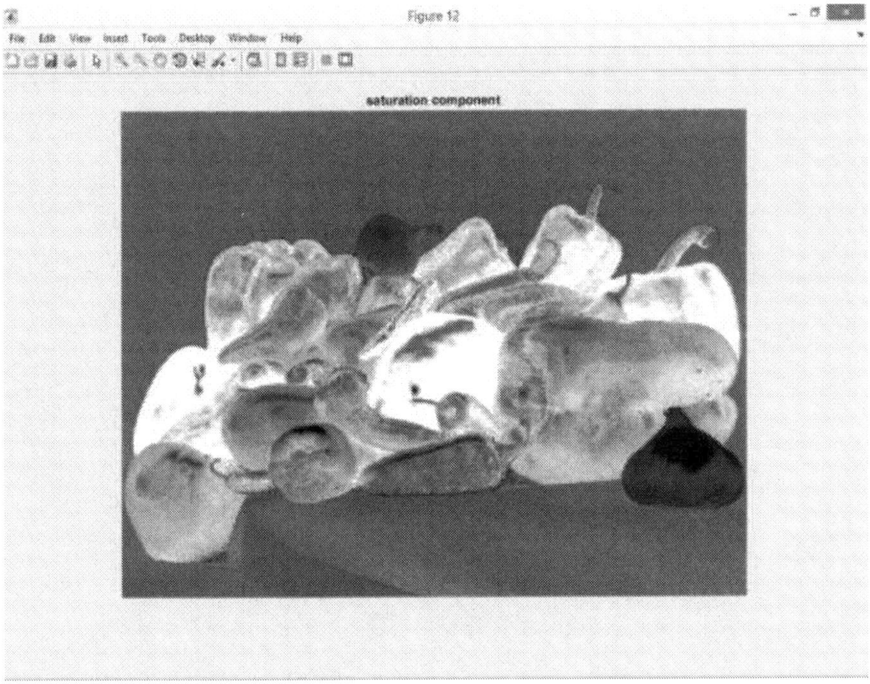
Figure 12
File Edit View Insert Tools Desktop Window Help
saturation component

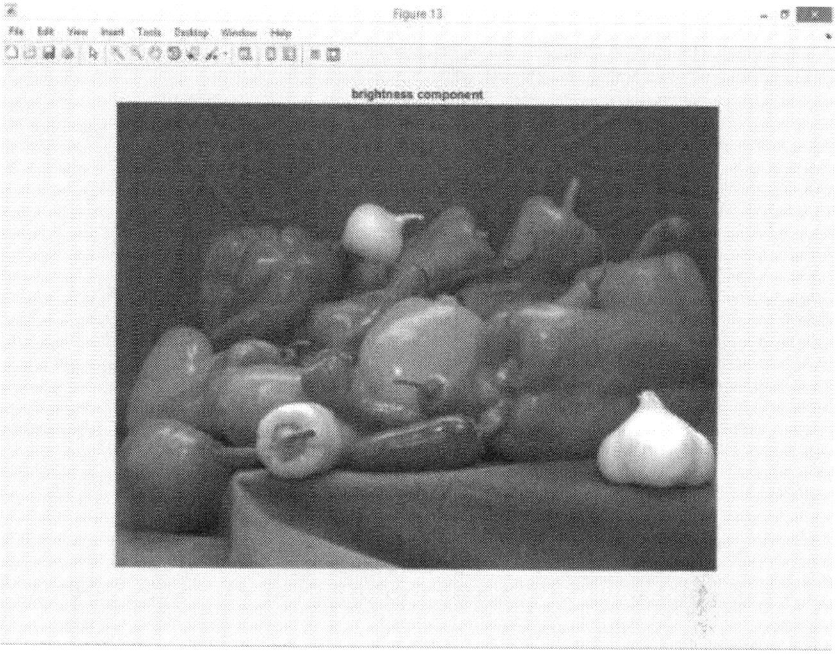
Figure 13
File Edit View Insert Tools Desktop Window Help
brightness component

# CHAPTER 9.

## DFT (DISCRETE FOURIER TRANSFORM) ANALYSIS

### Fourier Transform

The Fourier Transform is a significant image processing tool which is used to decompose an image into its sine and cosine components. The output of the conversion represents the image in the Fourier or frequency domain, though the input image is the spatial domain correspondent. Fourier domain image, each point signifies a particular frequency contained in the spatial domain image.

The Fourier Transform is used in a wide variety of applications, such as image filtering, image rebuilding, image compression and Image investigation

### Periodic Signals

A continuous-time signal x(t) is ***periodic*** if: $x(t + T) = x(t)$

**Fundamental period,**

$T_0$, of x(t) is smallest T satisfying above equation.

**Fundamental frequency**:

$f_0 = 1/T_0$

**Fundamental angular frequency**:

$\omega_0 = 2\pi/T_0 = 2\pi f_0$

$$x(t + T) = x(t)$$

***Fundamental frequency***:
$f_0 = 1/T_0$

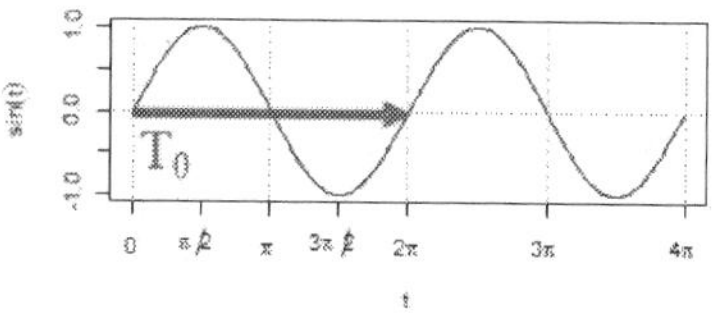


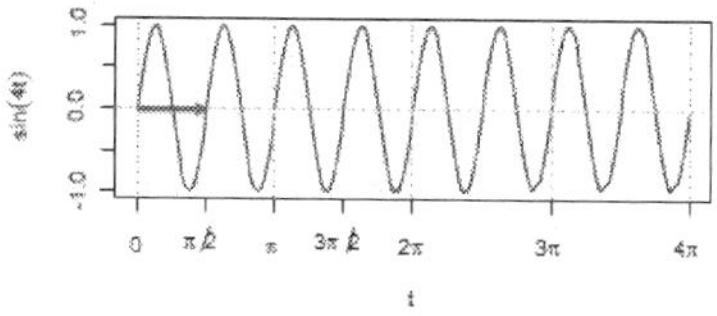


*Harmonics: Integer multiples of frequency of wave*

$$x(t + T) = x(t)$$

"Biological" Time Series

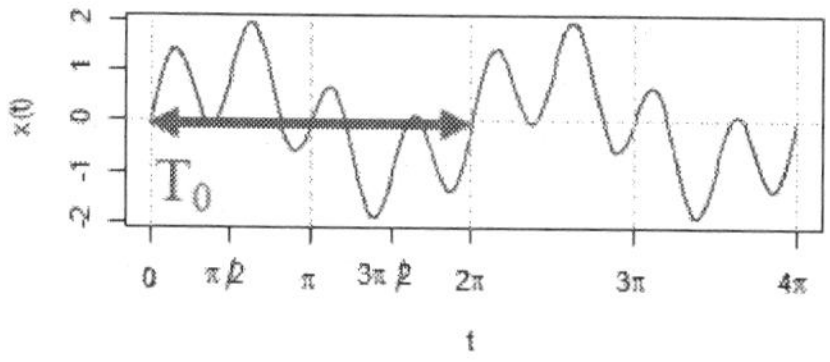


*Biological time series can be quite complex, and will contain noise.*

**Periodicity in Biology and Medicine**

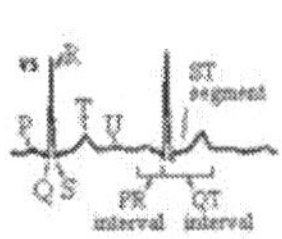


**Electrocardiogram (ECG):** Measure of the dipole moment produced by depolarization and repolarization of heart muscle cells.

**Somitogenesis:** A vertebrate's body plan: a segmented shape. Segmentation is recognized during somitogenesis, which is studied by Pourquie Lab.

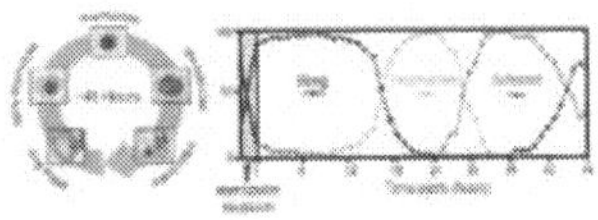

Intraerythrocytic Developmental Cycle of *Plasmodium falciparum*

X-Ray Computerized Tomography. Tomogram ("slice") produced by 2D FFT of digitally filtered x-ray data.

## Fourier analysis

### Fourier series

Expansion of continuous function into weighted sum of sins and cosines, or weighted sum of complex exponentials.

### Fourier Transform

Maps one function to another: continuous-to-continuous mapping, an integral transform.

### Discrete Fourier Transform (DFT)

Approximation to Fourier integral. Maps discrete vector to another discrete vector. Can be viewed as a matrix operator.

## Fast Fourier Transform (FFT)

Special computational algorithm for DFT.

| | Signal | Fourier transform unitary, angular frequency | Fourier transform unitary, ordinary frequency | Remarks |
|---|---|---|---|---|
| | $g(t) \equiv \frac{1}{\sqrt{2\pi}}\int_{-\infty}^{\infty} G(\omega)e^{i\omega t}d\omega$ | $G(\omega) \equiv \frac{1}{\sqrt{2\pi}}\int_{-\infty}^{\infty} g(t)e^{-i\omega t}dt$ | $G(f) \equiv \int_{-\infty}^{\infty} g(t)e^{-i2\pi ft}dt$ | |
| 1 | $a\cdot g(t)+b\cdot h(t)$ | $a\cdot G(\omega)+b\cdot H(\omega)$ | $a\cdot G(f)+b\cdot H(f)$ | Linearity |
| 2 | $g(t-a)$ | $e^{-ia\omega}G(\omega)$ | $e^{-i2\pi af}G(f)$ | Shift in time domain |
| 3 | $e^{iat}g(t)$ | $G(\omega-a)$ | $G\left(f-\frac{a}{2\pi}\right)$ | Shift in frequency domain, dual of 2 |
| 4 | $g(at)$ | $\frac{1}{\lvert a\rvert}G\left(\frac{\omega}{a}\right)$ | $\frac{1}{\lvert a\rvert}G\left(\frac{f}{a}\right)$ | If $\lvert a\rvert$ is large, then $g(at)$ is concentrated around 0 and $\frac{1}{\lvert a\rvert}G\left(\frac{\omega}{a}\right)$ spreads out and flattens |
| 5 | $G(t)$ | $g(-\omega)$ | $g(-f)$ | Duality property of the Fourier transform. Results from swapping "dummy" variables of $t$ and $\omega$. |
| 6 | $\frac{d^n g(t)}{dt^n}$ | $(i\omega)^n G(\omega)$ | $(i2\pi f)^n G(f)$ | Generalized derivative property of the Fourier transform |
| 7 | $t^n g(t)$ | $i^n \frac{d^n G(\omega)}{d\omega^n}$ | $\left(\frac{i}{2\pi}\right)^n \frac{d^n G(f)}{df^n}$ | This is the dual to 6 |
| 8 | $(g*h)(t)$ | $\sqrt{2\pi}G(\omega)H(\omega)$ | $G(f)H(f)$ | $g*h$ denotes the convolution of $g$ and $h$ — this rule is the convolution theorem |
| 9 | $g(t)h(t)$ | $\frac{(G*H)(\omega)}{\sqrt{2\pi}}$ | $(G*H)(f)$ | This is the dual of 8 |

## Discrete Fourier Transform (DFT):

**Forward 2D DFT**

$$F(u,v)=\frac{1}{MN}\sum_{x=0}^{M-1}\sum_{y=0}^{N-1} f(x,y)e^{-j2\pi(ux/M+vy/N)}$$

**Inverse 2D DFT**

$$f(x,y)=\sum_{u=0}^{M-1}\sum_{v=0}^{N-1} F(u,v)e^{-j2\pi(ux/M+vy/N)}$$

- (u, v) are the frequency coordinates while (x, y) are the spatial coordinates
- M, N are the number of spatial pixels along the x, y coordinates

## Fast Fourier Transform (FFT)

- The FFT is a computationally effectual algorithm to compute the Discrete Fourier Transform and its inverse.
- Assessing the sum above directly would take $O(N^2)$ arithmetic operations.
- The FFT algorithm decreases the computational burden to $O(N \log N)$ arithmetic operations.
- FFT needs the number of data points to be a power of 2 (usually 0 padding is used to make this true)
- FFT needs evenly-spaced time series

## Software

**FFTW**

www.fftw.org

FFTW is a C subroutine library for computing the discrete Fourier transform (DFT) in one or more dimensions, of arbitrary input size

**IDL** (see Signal Processing Demo for Fourier Filtering)

```
IDL> print, fft( [0,1,0,1] )
( 0.500000, 0.000000)( 0.000000, 0.000000)( -0.500000, 0.000000)( 0.000000, 0.000000)
```

**MatLab:** *Signal Processing/Image Processing Toolboxes*

```
>> fft( [0,1,0,1] )
ans =
     2     0    -2     0
```

**Mathematica:** *Perform symbolic or numerical Fourier analysis*

```
In[3]:= Fourier[{0, 1, 0, 1}]
Out[3]= {1. + 0. i, 0. + 0. i, -1. + 0. i, 0. + 0. i}
```

**R**

```
> fft( c(0,1,0,1) )
[1]  2+0i  0+0i -2+0i  0+0i
```

## DFT in MATLAB

Let *f* be a 2D image with dimension [M,N], then its 2D DFT can be computed as follows:

Df = fft2(f,M,N);

- fft2 puts the zero-frequency component at the top-left corner.
- fftshift Shifts the zero-frequency component to the center. (Useful for visualization.)

## MATLAB Program

```
f = imread('saturn.tif'); f = double(f);

Df = fft2(f,size(f,1), size(f,2));

figure; imshow(log(abs(Df)),[ ]);

Df2 = fftshift(Df);

figure; imshow(log(abs(Df2)),[ ]);
```

## Result

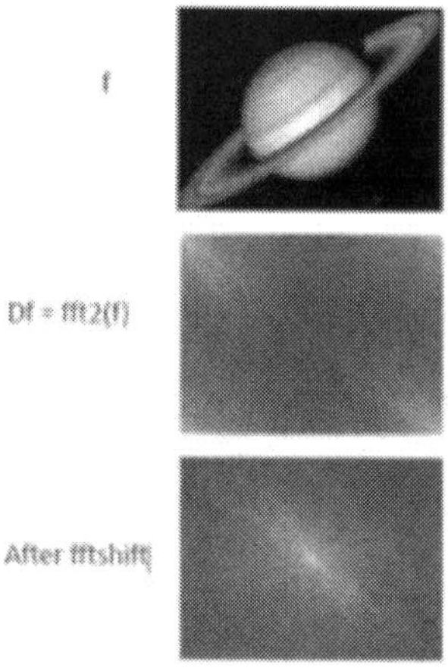

# DFT-Domain Filtering

```
a = imread('cameraman.tif');
Da = fft2(a);
Da = fftshift(Da);
figure; imshow(log(abs(Da)),[]);

H = zeros(256,256);
H(128-20:128+20,128-20:128+20) = 1;
figure; imshow(H,[]);

Db = Da.*H;
Db = fftshift(Db);
b = real(ifft2(Db));
figure; imshow(b,[]);
```

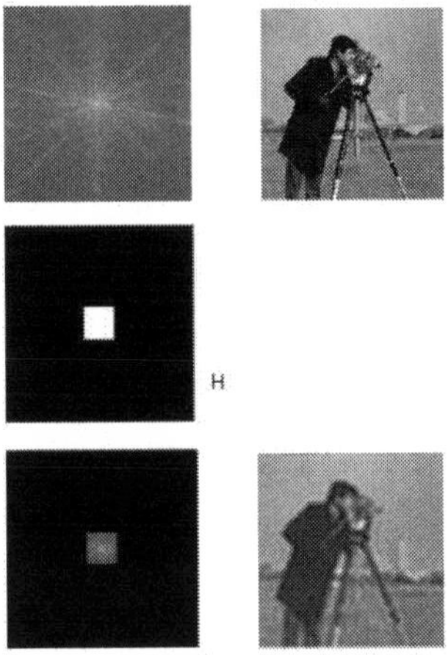


Frequency domain    Spatial domain

**Examine the Fourier transform of a synthetic image**

```
f = ones(10,20);

F = fft2(f, 500,500);

f1 = zeros(500,500);

f1(240:260,230:270) = 1;

subplot(2,2,1);

imshow(f1,[]);

S = abs(F);

subplot(2,2,2);

 imshow(S,[]);

Fc = fftshift(F);

S1 = abs(Fc);
```

```
subplot(2,2,3);
 imshow(S1,[]);
S2 = log(1+S1);
subplot(2,2,4);
imshow(S2,[]);
```

**Result**

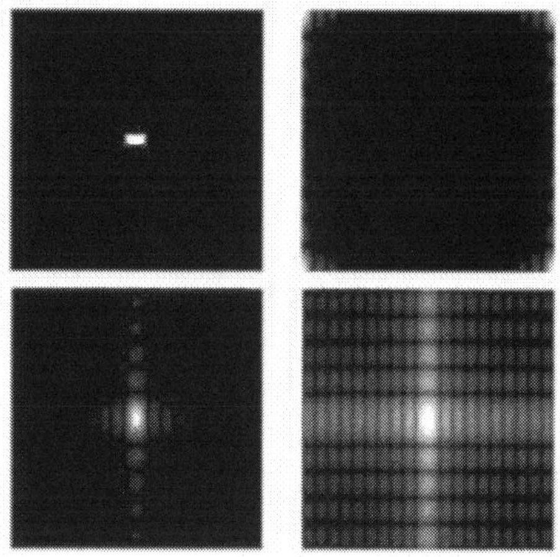

**Fourier transform of natural images**

```
f = imread('lenna.jpg');

subplot(1,2,1);

imshow(f);

f = double(f);

F = fft2(f);

Fc = fftshift(F);

S = log(1+abs(Fc));

Subplot(1,2,2);

imshow(S,[]);
```

**Result**

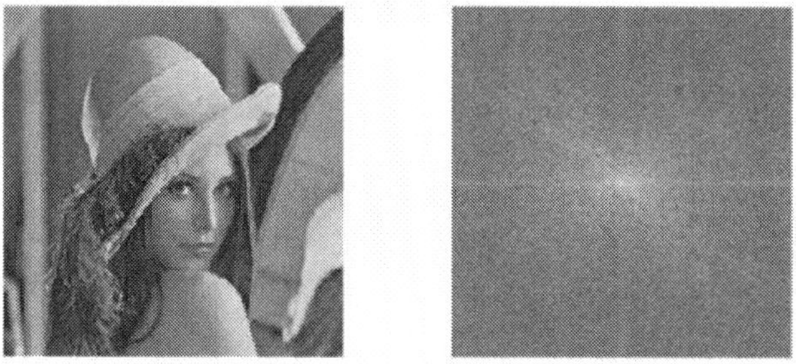

a. Original image

b. corresponding DFT image

## Application to image processing

- Cosine part → Directional blur operator
- Sine part → Directional Edge detector

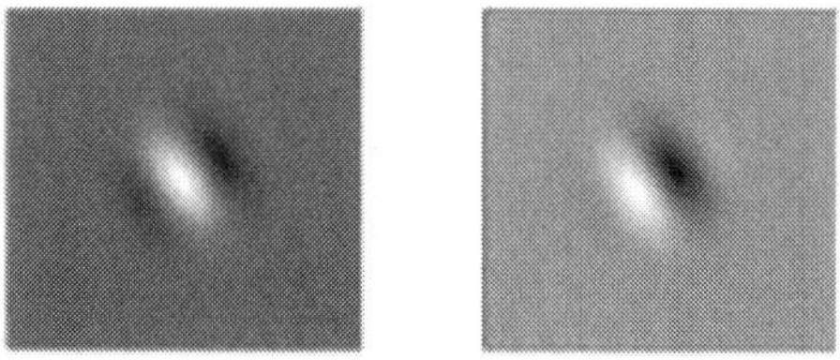

```
clc;

clear all;

close all;

a=zeros(256);

[m,n]=size(a);

for i=120:145

for j=120:145

   a(i,j)=225;

end;

end;

b=imrotate(a,45,'bilinear','crop');

a1=log(1+abs(fftshift(fft2(a))));

b1=log(1+abs(fftshift(fft2(b))));

subplot(2,2,1);

imshow(a);

title('Orignal Image');

subplot(2,2,2);

imshow(b);

title('Rotate Image');
```

```
subplot(2,2,3);

imshow(mat2gray(a1));

title('orignal image spectrum');

subplot(2,2,4);

imshow(mat2gray(b1));

title('spectrum of rotate img');
```

**RESULT**

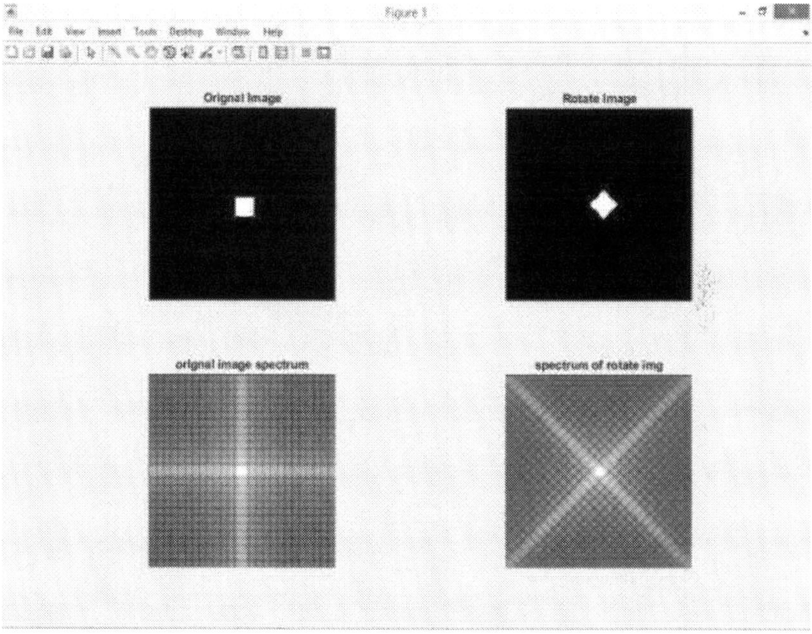

# CHAPTER 10.

## BASIC THRESHOLDING FUNCTION

### Thresholding

Thresholding is finding histogram of gray level intensity.

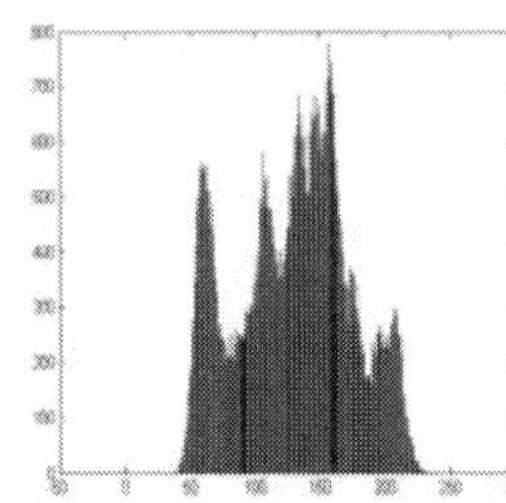

### Types

a) Basic Global Thresholding
b) Multiple Threshold
c) Variable Thresholding
d) Otsu's Method

### Basic Global Thresholding

- Initially Segment image use:

$$g(x, y) = \begin{cases} 1 & \text{if } f(x,y) \geq T \\ 0 & \text{if } f(x,y) \leq T \end{cases}$$

- Compute the average intensity **m1** and **m2** for the pixels

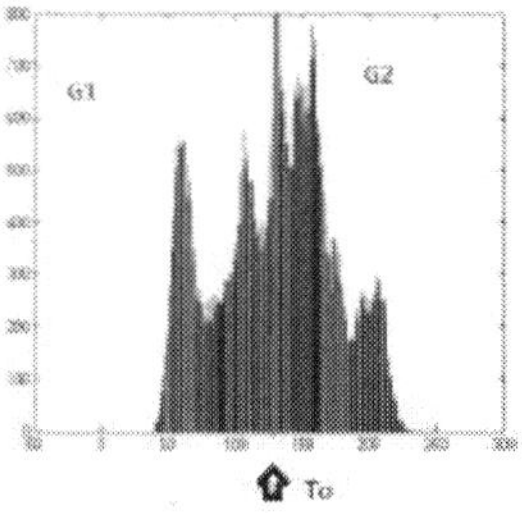


- Compute a new threshold:

$$T = \frac{1}{2}(m_1 + m_2)$$

- Until the difference between values of T is smaller than a predefined parameter.

## Global thresholding: an example

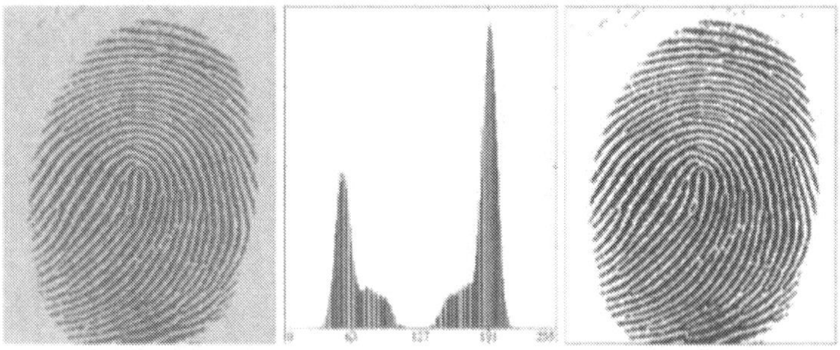

## Otsu's Method

- Based on a very simple idea: Find the threshold that minimizes the weighted within-class variance.
- This turns out to be the same as maximizing the between-class variance.
- Operates directly on the gray level histogram.

## Assumptions

- Histogram (and the image) are *bimodal.*
- No usage of *spatial coherence,* nor any other idea of object structure.
- Assumes stationary statistics, but can be modified to be locally adaptive. (exercises)
- Assumes uniform illumination (indirectly), so the bimodal illumination behavior arises from object appearance changes only.

Otsu's method: an example

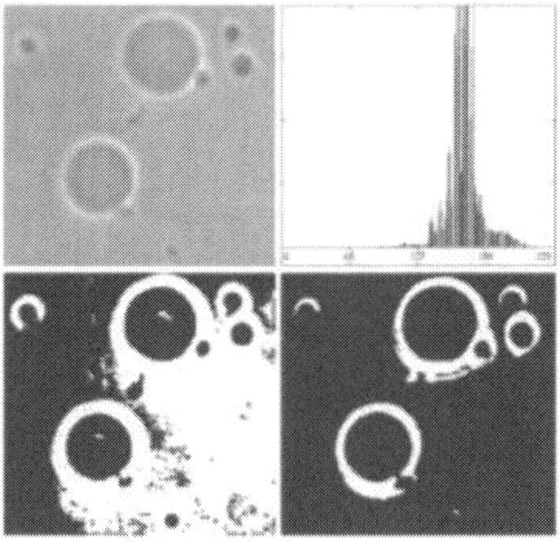

| a | b |
|---|---|
| c | d |

(a) original image; (b) histogram of (a); (c) global threshold: $T = 169$, $\eta = 0.467$; (d) Otsu's method: $T = 181$, $\eta = 0.944$.

**Multiple Threshold**

As Otsu's method, it takes more area and k*

$$\sigma_B^2 = P_1(m_1 - m_G)^2 + P_2(m_2 - m_G)^2 + P_3(m_3 - m_G)^2$$

$$P_1 m_1 + P_2 m_2 + P_3 m_3 = m_G$$

$$P_1 + P_2 + P_3 = 1$$

$$\sigma_B^2(k_1^*, k_2^*) = \max_{0 < k_1 < k_2 < L-1} \sigma_B^2(k_1, k_2)$$

$$\eta(k_1^*, k_2^*) = \frac{\sigma_B^2(k_1^*, k_2^*)}{\sigma_G^2}$$

**Disadvantage:**

It becomes too complex when number of area more than two or three.

## Watershed

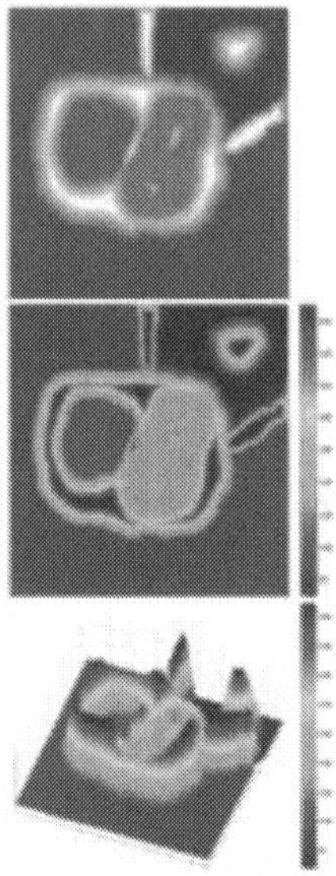

- The watershed technique is based on a topological interpretation of the image.
  - The intensity levels represent the height of the terrain that describe mountains and basins.
- For each basin, a hole in its minimum is supposed to be realized, from which, the rising underground water spills and fills the basins.
- As the water rises, the level reach the border of the basin and two or more adjacent basins tend to merge together.
- Dams are required for maintaining a separation between basins.
- These dams are the borders of the regions of the segmentation.

**Variable Thresholding**

- Image partitioning

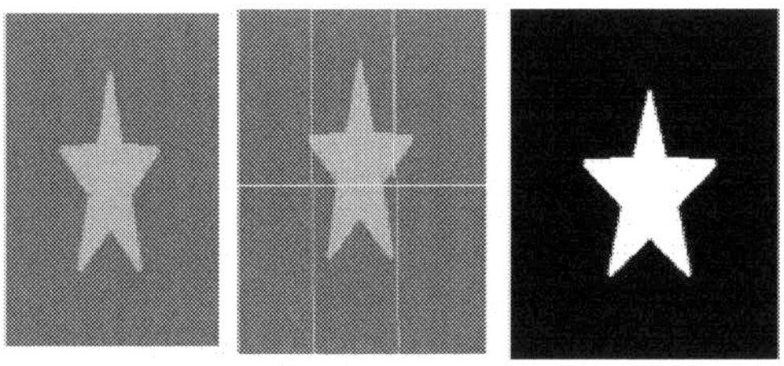

- It is work when the objects of interest and the background occupy regions of reasonably comparable size. If not, it will fail.
- Variable thresholding based on local image properties
- Using moving average
- It discussed is based on computing a moving average along scan lines of an image.

$$g(x, y) = \begin{cases} 1 & \text{if Q(local parameters) is true} \\ 0 & \text{if Q(local parameters) is true} \end{cases}$$

$$Q(\sigma_{xy}, m_{xy}) = \begin{cases} true & \text{if } f(x,y) > a\sigma_{xy} \text{ AND } f(x,y) > bm_{xy} \\ false & \text{otherwise} \end{cases}$$

## MATLAB Source Code For Basic Thresholding Function

```
clc;

clear all;

close all;

i=imread('cell.tif');

subplot(2,2,1);

imshow(i);

title('original image');

subplot(2,2,2);

im2bw(i,0.35);

title('mannual thershold image');

[counts,x]=imhist(i);

p=polyfit(x,counts,6);

y=polyval(p,x);

[v,ind]=sort(abs(diff(y)));

thresh=ind(3)./255;
```

```
subplot(2,2,3);

im2bw(i,thresh);

title(' polynomial thershold image');

level=graythresh(i);

subplot(2,2,4);

im2bw(i,level);

title('otsu method');

figure;

plot(x,counts);

hold on,plot(x,y,'r');

title('graph');
```

**RESULT**

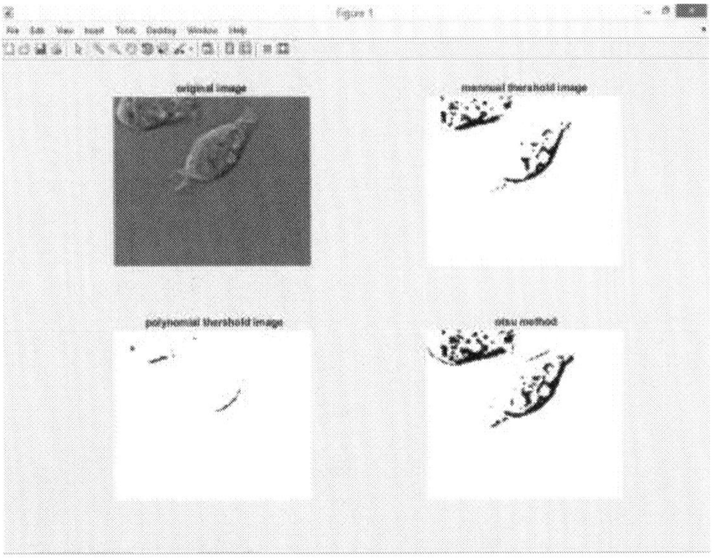

Figure 1
File Edit View Insert Tools Desktop Window Help
original image
mannual thershold image
polynomial thershold image
otsu method


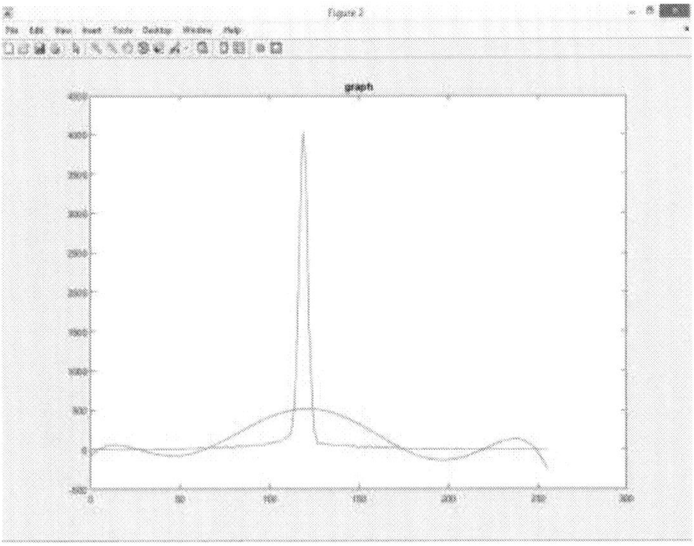

Figure 2
File Edit View Insert Tools Desktop Window Help
graph

MATLAB Code for Binary Thresholding Function & Histogram

```
clc;

clear all;

close all;

count=0;

a=imread('cell.tif');

t=mean2(a);

done=false;

while done

   count=count+1;

   g=f>t;

   tnext=0.5*(mean(f(g)));

   mean(a(~g));

   done=abs(t-tnext)<0.5;

   t=tnext;

end;

count=2;

t=125.3860;

g=im2bw(a,t/255);
```

```
subplot(2,2,1);

imshow(a);

title('original image');

subplot(2,2,2);

imhist(a);

title('histogram image');

subplot(2,2,3);

imshow(g);

title('binary image');
```

**OUTPUT**

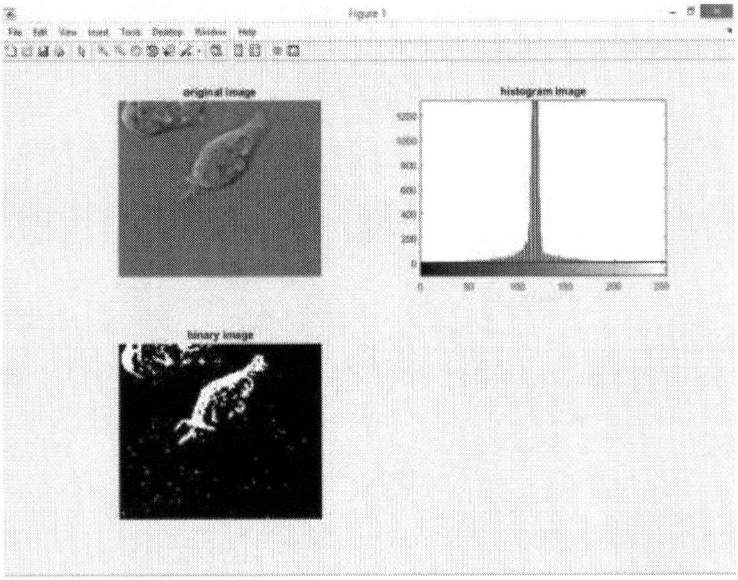

# CHAPTER 11.

# SAMPLING AND QUANTIZATION

## Image representation

An image is a *function* of the space.

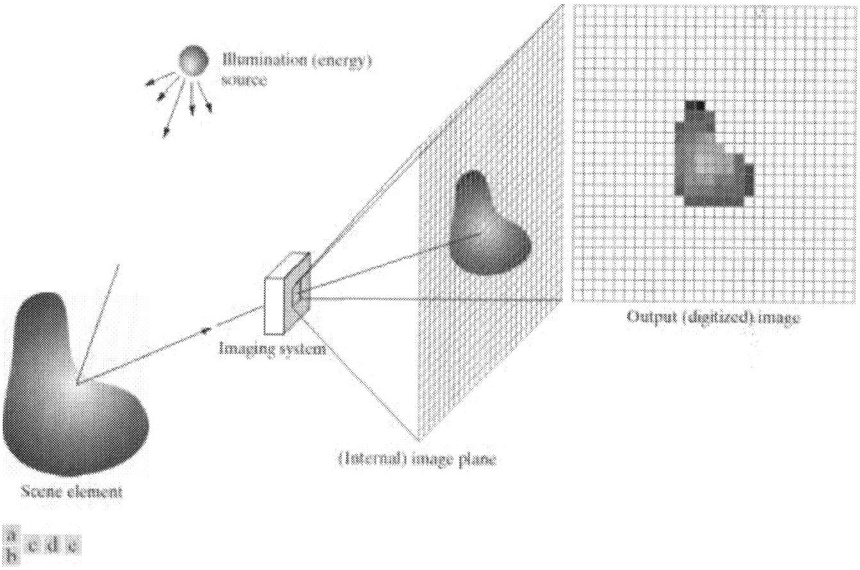


**FIGURE 2.15** An example of the digital image acquisition process. (a) Energy ("illumination") source. (b) An element of a scene. (c) Imaging system. (d) Projection of the scene onto the image plane. (e) Digitized image.

Typically, a 2-D projection of the 3-D space is used, but the image can exist in the 3-D space directly.

**Digitalization**

Digitalization of an analog signal involves two processes:

1. Sampling, and
2. Quantization.

Both processes correspond to a discretization of a quantity, but in different fields.

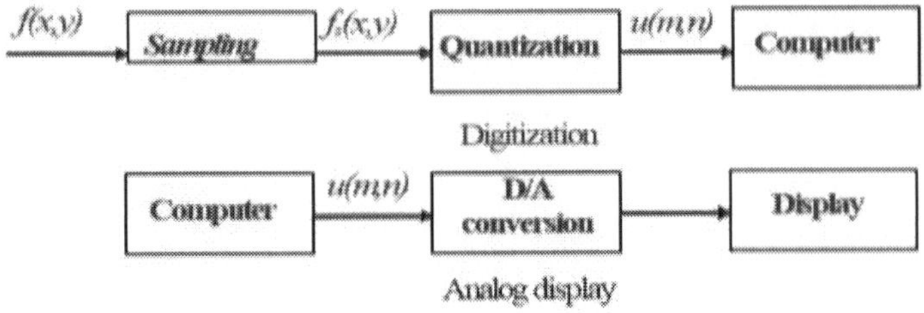


**Fig** Image sampling and quantization / Analog image display

**Sampling**

Sampling corresponds to a discretization of the space. That is, of the domain of the function, into f : $[1, \ldots, N] \times [1, \ldots, M] \longrightarrow R^m$.

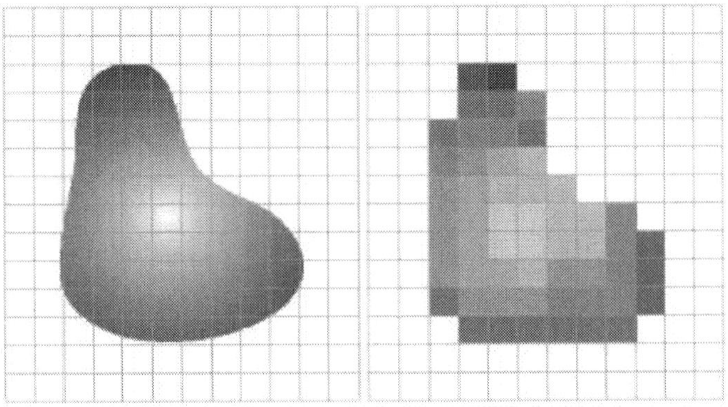

a b

FIGURE 2.17 (a) Continuous image projected onto a sensor array. (b) Result of image sampling and quantization.

## Quantization

Quantization corresponds to a discretization of the intensity values. That is, of the co-domain of the function.

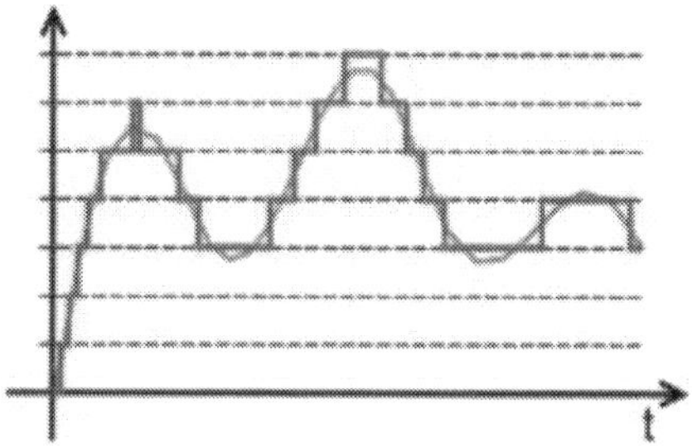


After sampling and quantization, we get

$f: [1, \ldots, N] \times [1, \ldots, M] \longrightarrow [0, \ldots, L].$

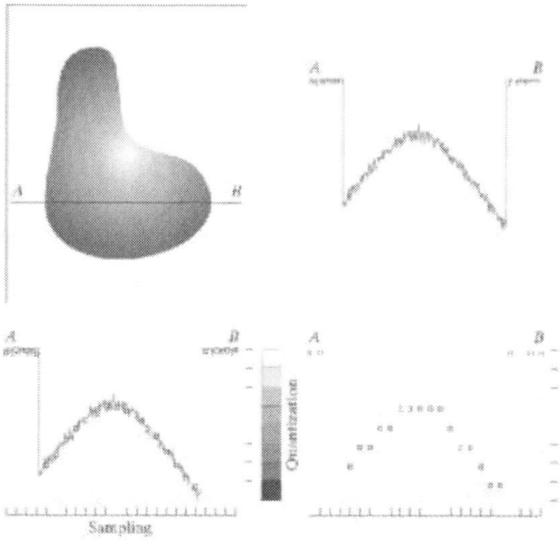


a b
c d

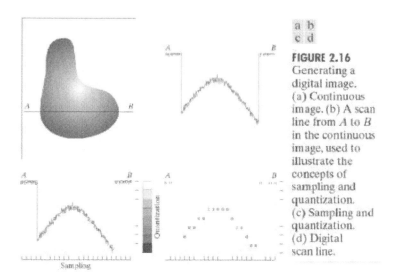

**FIGURE 2.16** Generating a digital image. (a) Continuous image. (b) A scan line from $A$ to $B$ in the continuous image, used to illustrate the concepts of sampling and quantization. (c) Sampling and quantization. (d) Digital scan line.

```
clc;

clear all;

close all;

a=imread('trees.tif');

f=ind2gray(a,gray(256));

f=f(1:256,1:256);

[N,M]=size(f);

m=7;

w=1/m;

F=fftshift(fft2(f));

for i=1:N

   for j=1:N

      r2=(i-round(N/2))^2+(j-round(N/2))^2;

      if(r2>round(N/2*w)^2)F(i,j)=0;

      end;

   end;

end;

Id=real(ifft2(fftshift(F)));
```

```
Id=imresize(Id,[N/m,N/m],'nearest');

m=10;

[N,M]=size(f);

Iu=zeros(m*N,m*N);

for i=1:N

   for j=1:N

       Iu(m*(i-1)+1,m*(j-1)+1)=f(i,j);

   end;

end;

[N,M]=size(Iu);

w=1/m;

F=fftshift(fft2(Iu));

for i=1:N

   for j=1:N

r2=(i-round(N/2))^2+(j-round(N/2))^2;

       if(r2>round(N/2*w)^2)F(i,j)=0;

       end;

   end;

end;

Iu=(m*m)*abs(ifft2(fftshift(F)));
```

```
figure;imshow(a);

title('original image');

figure;imshow(f);

title('gray image');

figure;imshow(Id);

title('Idown image');

figure;imshow(Iu);

title('Iup image');
```

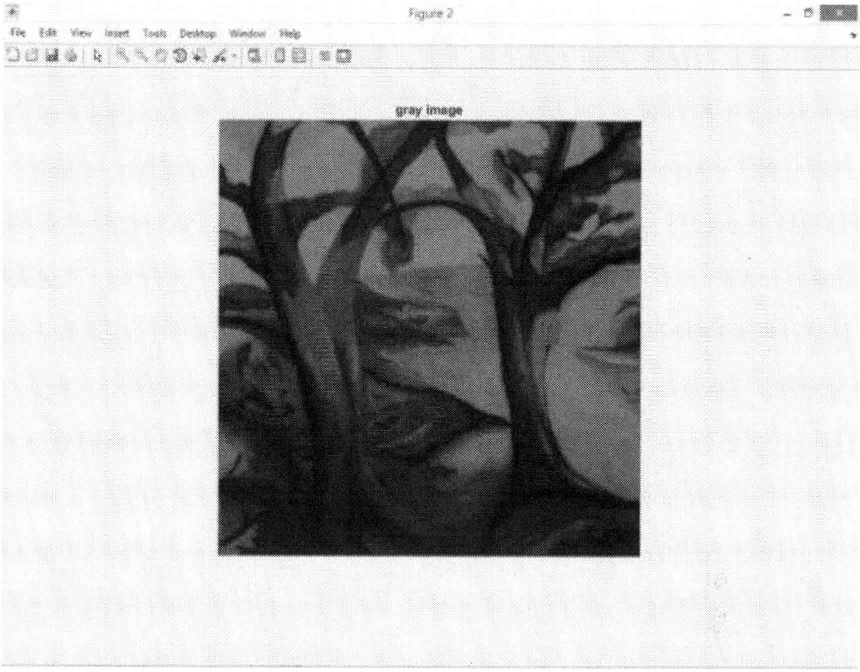
Figure 2
File Edit View Insert Tools Desktop Window Help
gray image

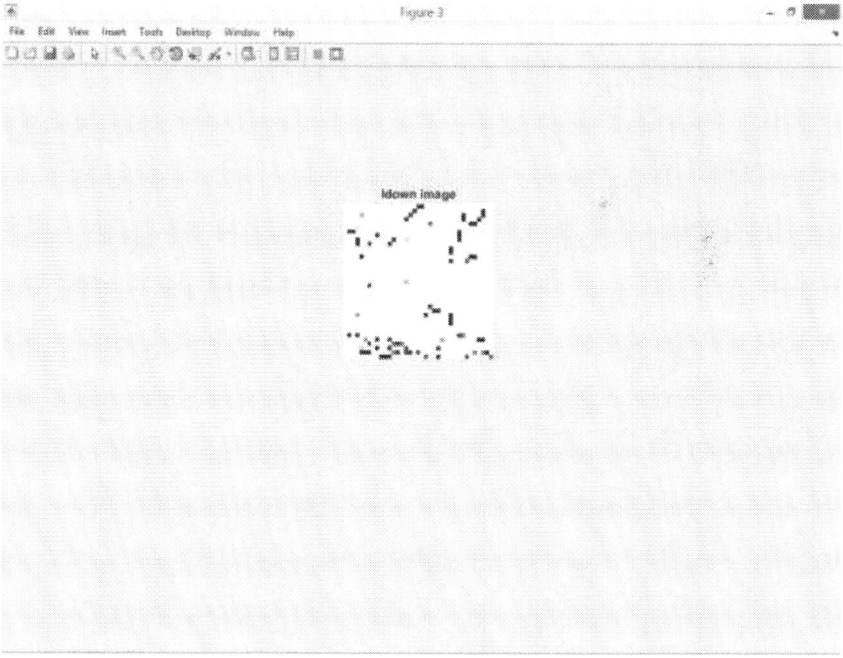
Figure 3
File Edit View Insert Tools Desktop Window Help
Idown image

Figure 4
File Edit View Insert Tools Desktop Window Help
lup image

# CHAPTER 12.

# IMAGE TRANSFORMATION

## Discrete Fourier Transform (DFT)

- The 2-D discrete Fourier transform of function f meant by F(u, v) is given by *F(u, v)* =∑ ∑ for u=0, 1, 2… M-1 and v=0, 1, 2… N-1
- The values F(u,v) are the DFT constants of f(x,y),
- The zero-frequency coefficients, F(0,0) is often called the 'DC component'.
- The MATLAB functions *fft, fft2* and *fftn* and their reverses *ifft, ifft2* and *ifftn* all use Fast Fourier Transform procedure to calculate DFT.
- DFT of a vector x of length n is another vector y of length n,

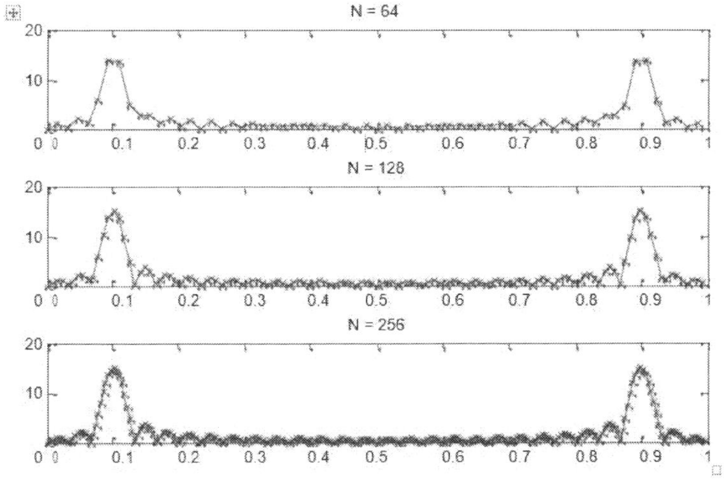


Fig: FFT Transformation

## 2. Discrete Cosine Transform (DCT)

DCT signifies an image as a sum of sinusoids of variable magnitude and frequencies. DCT has the property that, most of the info about the image is focused in just a few coefficients of DCT, for this aim DCT is used in compression.

**Example:**

DCT is at the heart of the world-wide standard lossy image compression algorithm known as JP

There are two ways to compute DCT using image processing toolbox, first method is to use *dct2* function, dct2 uses an FFT-based algorithm for quick computation with big inputs, The 2nd method is to use the DCT transform matrix, which is returned by the function dctmtx and might be more effectual for small square inputs, such as 8-by-8 or 16-by-16.

## WALSH HADAMARD TRANSFORM

Walsh Hadamard transform is a non-sinusoidal orthogonal transform method that decomposes a signal into set of basic functions. These functions are Walsh functions which are rectangular or square waves with +1 or -1.

***Hadamard function:***

- H=hadamard(n) returns hadamard matrix of order n.(n must be an integer and n,n/12 or n/20 must be a power of 2).
- Hadamard matrices are matrices of 1's and -1's whose columns are orthogonal.
- *Where [n n]=size(H) and I=eye(n,n);*{eye returns the identity matrix)
- Different ordering scheme are used to store Walsh function.That are: Sequency: coefficients in order of increasing sequence value. Hadamard: coefficient in hadamard order.
- Dyadic: coefficient in gray code order.

**Application of Walsh hadamard transform:**

- ✓ Speech processing,
- ✓ filtering and
- ✓ power spectrum analysis.

Walsh-hadamard transform has a fast version *fwht* (fast Walsh-hadamard transform). Compare to fft, fwht requires less storage space and is faster to calculate because it uses real addition and subtraction while fft requires complex calculation. Inverse of fwht is *ifwht.*

**Definition of IFWHT:**

- *Y=fwht(X)* returns the coefficient of the discrete Walsh Hadamard transform.
- *Y=fwht(X,n)* returns the n-point discrete Walsh hadamard transform,nmust be power of 2.X and n must be of same length.If X is longer than n,X is truncate and if X is shorter than n,X is padded with zeros.
- *Y=fwht(X,n,ordering)* specifies the ordering to use for the returned Walsh-hadamard transform coefficient.

**Applications of Transforms**

- feature extraction and representation
- Enhancement and Compression
- pattern recognition,e.g.,eigen faces
  dimensionality reduction
- Analyse the principal ("dominating") components

**Radon transform**

- The Radon transform of a two dimensional function, *f(x,y)* is the line integral of *f* parallel to the $y'$-axis given by
- The radon function computes projections of an image matrix along specified directions. It computes the line integral from multiple source along parallel paths, or beams, in a certain direction. The beams are spaced 1 pixel unit apart. To represent an image, radon function takes multiple, parallel-beam projections of the image from different angles by rotating the source around the center of the image

## MATLAB Source Code For Image Transformation

```
clc;
clear all;
close all;
a=imread('mri.tif');
figure,imshow(uint8(a));
title('original image');
a=double(a);
[s1,s2]=size(a);
bs=8;
%waslh matrix
hadamardMatrix=hadamard(bs);
M=log2(bs)+1;
hadIdx=0:bs-1;
binhadIdx=fliplr(dec2bin(hadIdx,M))-'0';
binseqIdx=zeros(bs,M-1);
for k=M:-1:2
   binseqIdx(:,k)=xor(binhadIdx(:,k),binhadIdx(:,k-1));
end;
```

```
seqIdx=binseqIdx*pow2((M-1:-1:0)');
walshMatrix=hadamardMatrix(seqIdx+1,:);
%walsh
temp_walsh=double(zeros(size(a)));
for y=1:bs:s1-bs+1
  for x=1:bs:s2-bs+1
    croppedImage=a((y:y+bs-1),(x:x+bs-1));
    h=walshMatrix;
    m=log2(bs);
    t=(1/(2^m))*h*croppedImage*h';
    temp_walsh((y:y+bs-1),(x:x+bs-1))=t;
  end;
end;
figure(2),subplot(1,2,1);
imshow(uint8(temp_walsh));
title('walsh transform  image');
%inverse walsh
temp_inwalsh=double(zeros(size(a)));
for y=1:bs:s1-bs+1
  for x=1:bs:s2-bs+1
    croppedImage=temp_walsh((y:y+bs-1),(x:x+bs-1));
    h=walshMatrix;
```

```
    m=log2(bs);
    t=(1/(2^m))*h*croppedImage*h;
    %t=getInwalshtransform(croppedImage,bs);
    temp_inwalsh((y:y+bs-1),(x:x+bs-1))=t;
  end;
end;
subplot(1,2,2);
imshow(uint8(temp_inwalsh));
title('inverse walsh transform image');
%hadamard
temp=double(zeros(size(a)));
for y=1:bs:s1-bs+1
  for x=1:bs:s2-bs+1
    croppedImage=a((y:y+bs-1),(x:x+bs-1));
    N=bs;
    h=hadamard(N);
    m=log2(N);
    t=(1/(2^m))*h*croppedImage*h';
    %t=getInwalshtransform(croppedImage,bs);
    temp((y:y+bs-1),(x:x+bs-1))=t;
  end;
end;
```

```
figure(3),subplot(1,2,1);
imshow(uint8(temp));
title('hadamard transform  image');
%inverse hadamard
temp1=double(zeros(size(a)));
for y=1:bs:s1-bs+1
  for x=1:bs:s2-bs+1
    croppedImage=temp((y:y+bs-1),(x:x+bs-1));
    h=hadamard(N);
    m=log2(N);
    t=(1/(2^m))*h'*croppedImage*h;
    %t=getInvhadamardtransform(croppedImage,bs);
    temp1((y:y+bs-1),(x:x+bs-1))=t;
  end;
end;
subplot(1,2,2);
imshow(uint8(temp1));
title('inverse hadamard transform image');
%dct
temp_dct=double(zeros(size(a)));
for y=1:bs:s1-bs+1
  for x=1:bs:s2-bs+1
```

```
    croppedImage=a((y:y+bs-1),(x:x+bs-1));
    s=dctmtx(N);
    t=s*croppedImage*s';
    %t=getdcttransform(croppedImage,bs);
    temp_dct((y:y+bs-1),(x:x+bs-1))=t;
  end;
end;
figure(4),subplot(1,2,1);
imshow(uint8(temp_dct));
title('dct transform image');
%inverse dct
temp_invdct=double(zeros(size(a)));
for y=1:bs:s1-bs+1
  for x=1:bs:s2-bs+1
    croppedImage=temp_dct((y:y+bs-1),(x:x+bs-1));
    s=dctmtx(N);
    t=s'*croppedImage*s;
    %t=getInvdcttransform(croppedImage,bs);
    temp_invdct((y:y+bs-1),(x:x+bs-1))=t;
  end;
end;
subplot(1,2,2);
```

```
imshow(uint8(temp_invdct));

title('inverse dct transform image');

%haar matrix

a=1/sqrt(N);

for i=1:N

  H(1,i)=a;

end;

for k=1:N-1

  p=fix(log2(k));

  q=k-2^p+1;

  t1=N/2^p;

  sup=fix(q*t1);

  mid=fix(sup-t1/2);

  inft=fix(sup-t1);

  t2=2^(p/2)*a;

  for j=1:inft

    H(k+1,j)=0;

  end;

  for j=inft+1:mid

    H(k+1,j)=t2;

  end;

  for j=mid+1:sup
```

```
    h(k+1,j)=-t2;
  end;
  for j=sup+1:N
    H(k+1,j)=0;
  end;
end;
%haar
temp_haar=double(zeros(size(a)));
for y=1:bs:s1-bs+1
  for x=1:bs:s2-bs+1
    croppedImage=a((y:y+bs-1),(x:x+bs-1));
    h=H;
    m=log2(N);
    t=h*croppedImage*h';
    %t=gethaartransform(croppedImage,bs);
    temp_haar((y:y+bs-1),(x:x+bs-1))=t;
  end;
end;
figure(5),subplot(1,2,1);
imshow(unit8(temp_haar));
title('haar transform image');
%inverse haar
```

```
temp_invhaar=double(zeros(size(a)));
for y=1:bs:s1-bs+1
  for x=1:bs:s2-bs+1
    croppedImage=temp_haar((y:y+bs-1),(x:x+bs-1));
    h=H;
    t=h'*croppedImage*h;
    %t=getInvhaartransform(croppedImage,bs);
    temp_invhaar((y:y+bs-1),(x:x+bs-1))=t;
  end;
end;
subplot(1,2,2);
imshow(unit8(temp_invhaar));
title('inverse haar transform image');
```

**OUTPUT FOR IMAGE TRANSFORMATION**

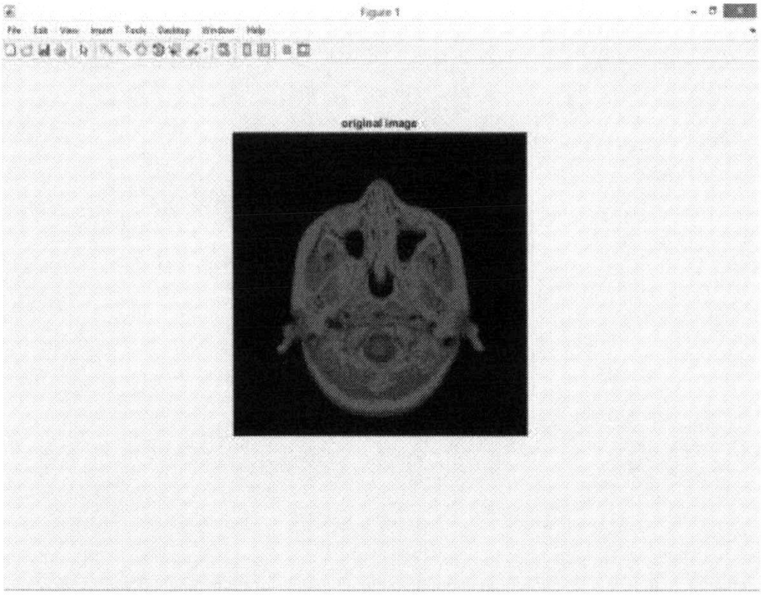


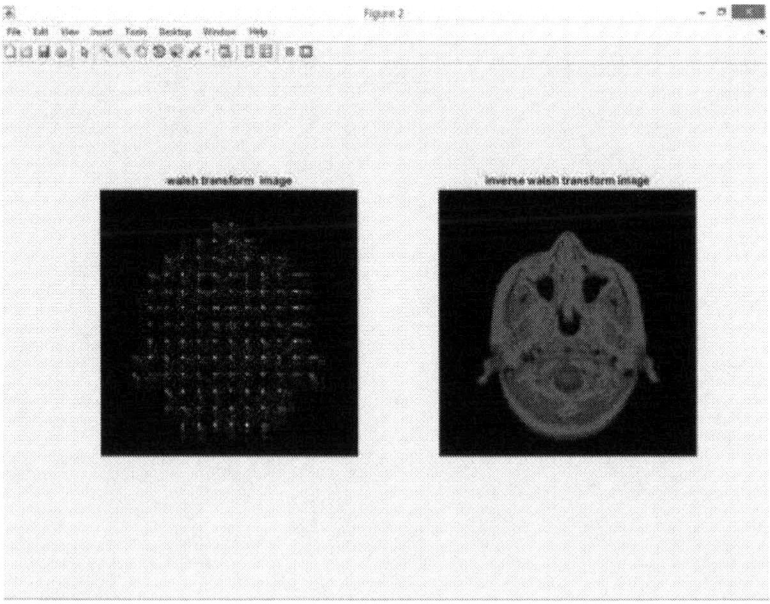

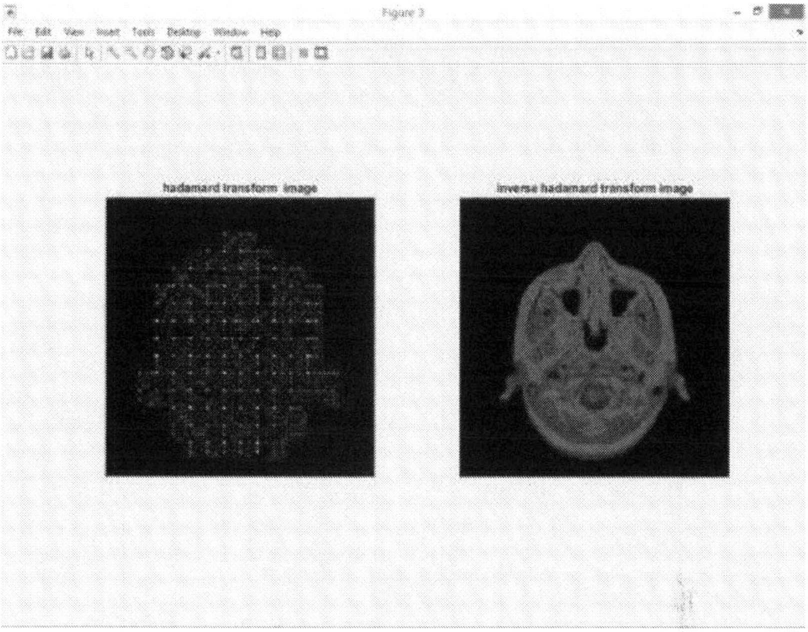
Figure 3
File Edit View Insert Tools Desktop Window Help
hadamard transform image
inverse hadamard transform image

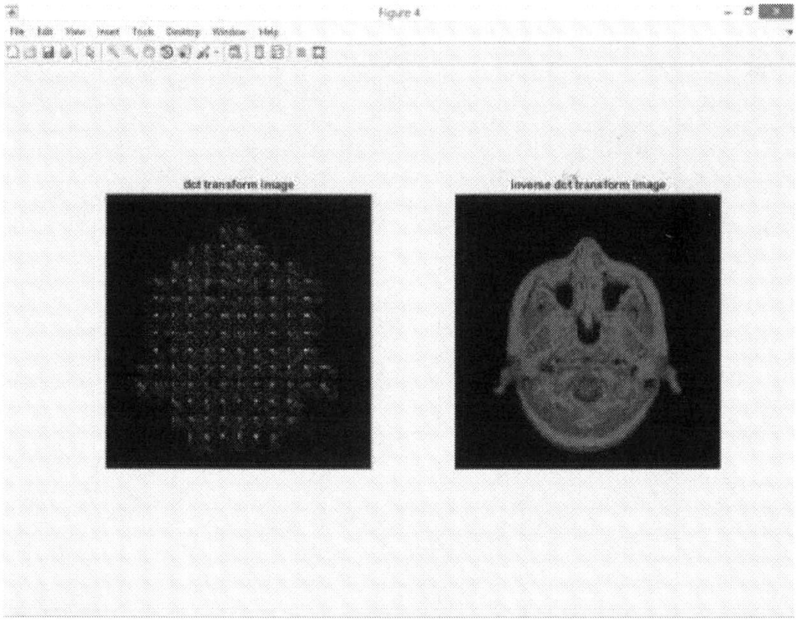
Figure 4
File Edit View Insert Tools Desktop Window Help
dct transform image
inverse dct transform image

# APPENDIX

**Top 100+ Image Processing Projects - Free Source Code and Abstracts**

https://www.pantechsolutions.net/blog/category/image-video-processing/amp/

https://www.pantechsolutions.net/blog/top-100-image-processing-projects-free-source-code/amp/

**Basic Image Processing Projects**

https://electronicsforu.com/electronics-projects/software-projects-ideas/image-processing-using-matlab

**Official Image Processing References**

https://in.mathworks.com/discovery/digital-image-processing.html

**MATLAB Official Images Processing Toolbox Link**

https://in.mathworks.com/products/image.html

**Example Codes for Image Processing**

https://in.mathworks.com/products/image/code-examples.html

**If u don't have MATLAB software please Purchase from this link**

https://in.mathworks.com/store

**REFERENCE:**


[1] Kenneth R. Castleman. Digital Image Processing. Prentice Hall, 1996.

[2] Ashley R. Clark and Colin N Eberhardt. Microscopy Techniques for Materials Science. CRC Press, Boca Raton, Fl, 2002.

[3] Rafael Gonzalez and Richard E. Woods. Digital Image Processing. Addison-Wesley, second edition, March, 2017.

[4] Robert M. Haralick and Linda G. Shapiro. Computer and Robot Vision. Addison-Wesley, 1993.

[5] James D. Foley, Andries van Dam, Steven K. Feiner, John F. Hughes, and Richard L. Phillips. Introduction to Computer Graphics. Addison-Wesley, 1994.

[6] Robert V. Hogg and Allen T. Craig. Introduction to Mathematical Statistics. Prentice-Hall, f ifth edition, 1994.

[7] William K. Pratt. Digital Image Processing. John Wiley and Sons, second edition, 1991.

[8] Jae S. Lim. Two-Dimensional Signal and Image Processing. Prentice Hall, 1990.

[9] Majid Rabbani and Paul W. Jones. Digital Image Compression Techniques. SPIE Optical Engineering Press, 1991.

[10] Jean Paul Serra. Image analysis and mathematical morphology. Academic Press, 1982.

[11] Steven Roman. Introduction to Coding and Information Theory. Springer-Verlag, 1997.

[12] Azriel Rosenfeld and Avinash C. Kak. Digital Picture Processing. Academic Press, second edition, 1982.

[13] Melvin P. Siedband. Medical imaging systems. In John G. Webster, editor, Medical instrumentation : application and design, pages 518–576. John Wiley and Sons, 1998.

[14] Milan Sonka, Vaclav Hlavac, and Roger Boyle. Image Processing, Analysis and Machine Vision. PWS Publishing, second edition, 1999.

[15] Dominic Welsh. Codes and Cryptography. Oxford University Press, 1989.

[16] Scott E. Umbaugh. Computer Vision and Image Processing: A Practical Approach Using CVIPTools. Prentice-Hall, 1998.

[17] https://www.pantechsolutions.net/blog/category/image-video-processing/amp/

[18] https://www.pantechsolutions.net/blog/top-100-image-processing-projects-free-source-code/amp/

[19] https://in.mathworks.com/discovery/digital-image-processing.html

# About The Author

Arsath Natheem is an indian Biomedical Engineer and Youtuber who works primarily in the field of Artificial intelligence, He is best known for his multimedia Presentation about "How the Biomedical Engineers Save the life" at Velalar College of Engineering and Technology in Tamilnadu, he was awarded the best project holder for IoT Based Voice Recognition Robot and also presented his project at Adhiyamaan college of engineering and Technology and won the first prize for his project. He participated project competition at Madras institute of technology (MIT) in Chennai, now he pursuing final year BE Biomedical Engineering at Velalar College of Engineering and Technology, He's field of interest is an Artificial Intelligence it's specifically applicable for Medical Diagnosis.

## ONE LAST THING...

If you enjoyed this book or found it useful I'd be very grateful if you'd post a short review on Amazon. Your support really does make a difference and I read all the reviews personally so I can get your feedback and make this book even better.

If you'd like to leave a review then all you need to do is click the review link on this book's page on Amazon here: http://amzn.to/2jXcHfL

Thanks again for your support!

Made in the USA
San Bernardino, CA
10 January 2020

62996592R00141